PRACTICAL SCR

A User's Guide

Heath H. Herel

Table of Contents

Preface - Something Witty This Way Comes

Scrum (n): a lightweight framework that helps people, teams and organizations generate value through adaptive solutions for complex problems.[i]

I've written a lot of words over the last 10 years or so about Scrum. I have talked about Scrum at work, at home, and even on the set of Jeopardy! when asked by Alex Trebek what a Scrum Master is. I've been told I am a walking commercial for Scrum. Like many of you reading this, I believe in Scrum to my very core. I have seen what it can do when it works, and how it can transform the way we work into something exciting and dynamic. I have also seen my share of problems and challenges arise. I have attended classes and conferences, and taken numerous certification exams to challenge myself and verify (to myself) that I have gained the knowledge I desire.

In my blog I have written about many of my personal observations (and I will undoubtedly continue to do so), and you will find the genesis of many parts of this book in my blog. Some of it is copied here almost word for word. It is these very observations that drove me to write this book to talk about what works and what doesn't from my own perspective; not from the perspective of a professional trainer or consultant, but from someone who is in the trenches with Scrum Teams on a daily basis.

Not everything in here will apply to you, to your situation, or to your organization. There might even be things I have written here that you strongly disagree with. That's cool. I don't think anyone can write a book with personal insights and tips that will be all things to all readers. Hopefully, you can find something in here that does appeal to you and that provides guidance or makes you think a little bit.

If you pull only two things from this book, let it be these:
- **Do what is right for your team.**
- **When in doubt, ask your team.**

What works perfectly for one team might not for another. It is important that we are as Agile as we want our teams to be. Don't be afraid to experiment and see what works. I tell everyone that we can try anything for a Sprint or three and see if it works for us. It is through this constant experimentation, and a frequent Inspect and Adapt cycle, that we transform how we work and truly gain the benefits of Agile. Don't be afraid to get outside of your own comfort zone, and don't be afraid to have FUN. Specific tactics for how you use the Scrum framework can, and should, vary based on what your team requires. While it is important that you don't leave out parts of Scrum, it's also important that you aren't acting as the Scrum police and enforcing every little thing along the way. The Scrum Team needs room to breathe and find what is going to work best for them.

Ultimately, the best way to know what's right for your Scrum Team is often to simply ask them. There's something you want to have them try to do? Ask them. There's a question about whether something extra can be done in the current Sprint? Ask them. You want to get ice cream or craft beers for the team and don't know what to buy? Ask them. Not all questions have to be serious, business-oriented ones, after all. Trust your team. They know what is best for them.

You absolutely have to do everything that is in the Agile framework your organization is using. That's important. But what makes a difference and makes your teams truly Agile is the understanding of why it is important. This book is focused on Scrum because that's where my expertise lies, but much of what is here applies to any Agile framework your team(s) might be using. It's also critical to recognize that you can't just keep working in the same old ways but use the Scrum terminology, because nothing will change. Scrum is not about micromanaging your teams; it relies on empowering your teams and letting them make the right choices for your product.

This book is intentionally short and written in brief easily-digestible sections. Feel free to skip around and find the parts that are important to you. This isn't a Scrum 101 book, but there are definitely pieces here that focus on what to do. Hopefully what follows will help guide you as to why we do it.

What to expect

Chapter I - Introduction discusses whether we are Doing Agile or Being Agile and the important difference between the two. Here we also meet the Team we will be working with periodically throughout the course of this book.

Chapter II - A Tale of Three Transformations recounts an actual Agile Transformation that I was an integral part of. There were mistakes made and lessons learned, and much of what happened and is shared here sets the stage for the rest of this book, as it did for my career in Scrum.

Chapter III - Bringing the Scrum Values to Life takes a dive into each of the five Scrum Values (Commitment, Courage, Focus, Openness, Respect) and examines how the values work together to build a strong foundation upon which Scrum itself depends.

Chapter IV - Scrum at Me, Bro! examines the basics of Scrum. It looks at the empirical process, the basic 3-5-3 structure, and how things like our Definition of Done and how we handle defects play a large role in our success as a Scrum Team.

Chapter V - What's the Plan looks at all of the planning elements of Scrum, from the Daily Scrum to Sprint and Release Planning. It discusses how we use Sprint Goals, debunks some of the myths surrounding planning, and addresses how to handle a situation where we don't quite get everything done that we forecast.

Chapter VI - In My Estimation digs into how we estimate in Scrum from hours to Story Points, and how vague estimates are more accurate than precise ones. It introduces a game useful for teaching teams how to estimate and breaks down some of the myths surrounding velocity. It also includes a bit about not estimating at all and how that might work better for your teams.

Chapter VII - Retrospectively Speaking is all about Sprint Retrospectives. I cover what is in my toolkit to run a great Retrospective, advise how to keep your retrospectives fresh, and provide examples of a couple of very different actual Retrospectives I have run with my teams.

Chapter VIII - Building a Better... examines each of the three Roles in Scrum, in depth, with thoughts and ideas strictly focused on what makes a great member in each of those roles. It gets into detail as to how the roles work together to build amazing Scrum Teams.

Chapter IX - Coaching and Collaboration gets deeper into specific skills and thoughts surrounding how to be a better coach and facilitator. While this is largely aimed at the Scrum Master, there is ample material here for anyone looking to be a better coach.

Chapter X - Leveling Up: Ding! focuses on challenges you might encounter and thoughts on how to handle those challenges as they arise. This is all about getting even better at what you do and brings the book to a close by challenging you to find your own ways to achieve growth.

x

I - Introduction

"If you dislike change, you're going to dislike irrelevance even more" - Gen. Eric Shinseki

Doing or Being?

Something came up a while ago that got me thinking:
I heard someone use the phrase "We do Agile..."

The rest of the sentence is irrelevant. This phrase says everything.

Like a lot of people, I have teams who are at varying levels of success with Scrum. Some teams are all in and it shows, where others are struggling. What hit me is that this phrase cuts right to the heart of the problem. Are we Agile, or are we merely "doing" Agile?

There is, clearly, a world of difference between these two.

When I heard someone say this, I started asking myself some questions:

- Are we going through the motions of being Agile while simultaneously resisting the change that needs to happen to achieve real success?
- Is there a perception that Agile is just a fad/phase?
- Is there an understanding of what we are doing, or did someone just hit on a buzzword and decide that we needed to try this?
- Do we have top-down support from executive leadership to change the culture?

In my case, I took this as an opportunity to start a conversation to gain an understanding of what the speaker meant and see if there was a coaching opportunity in front of me. There was, as it turned out. This person was never actually trained and just started doing what the Scrum Master said they had to do without a full appreciation of why it was all being done. A few minutes of conversation later I could see the light starting to go on and this person starting to move away from doing and on to being.

Scrum is not just a turnkey solution that will fix all of the problems the organization is facing. You can't walk in one morning, flip a switch and suddenly become an Agile workplace. It requires a great deal of work from the top down to not only commit to doing everything that Scrum dictates, but to fundamentally change the culture and embrace the change Scrum requires. It is important that we always keep in mind that Scrum is a framework, not a methodology. If we are only going through the motions of doing the things in the Scrum Guide without making the corresponding changes to our organization, we cannot truly be Agile. I have seen where this highly modified and bastardized version of Scrum fails. I had a front row seat during the first Agile transformation I was ever a part of. The belief was that just doing the events of Scrum would transform our way of working. It did not.

Scrum requires a transformational shift in your organization. Teams need to be fully empowered in how they work, and entrusted with the knowledge and confidence that they will make the right decisions when creating a product. The Product Owner is given absolute authority over her product, with the power to drive value forward at all times. Scrum Masters are there not to enforce the rules, but to coach, mentor, and facilitate the changes required by Scrum.

Scrum is not a prescriptive set of best practices that will automatically transform your team overnight. It requires a lot of hard work. If you read the Scrum Guide carefully, you will notice that there are actually no practices in place for how your organization should make Scrum work. It merely lays out the framework upon which you build highly productive teams and highly valuable products.

When Scrum fails, it is not because the framework is flawed, it is because we, as an organization, have not done our part to allow it to succeed. When Scrum is struggling, look at what is happening and identify the root cause. Is the Product Owner frequently overruled on her decisions by upper management, or is she given complete autonomy? Is the Scrum Master just there to be a secretary for the Scrum Team, merely to keep the board up to date and be the Scrum police? Are the Developers fully empowered with how to create the product, or are decisions being made for them and they are there merely to do exactly what they are told? Does the team still require the Business Requirements Document before they proceed, or are they collaborating to refine requirements and engineer a proper solution? Are managers actively involved with every single detail the team is working on, or have they taken a step back to become leaders, actively working to empower their teams and give them the tools they need for success?

I thought back to the first Agile transformation I was a part of and the reasons it failed so horribly. One of the key reasons (in hindsight) is that we were simply told that now we were Agile and "DO THIS," without actually getting us to understand WHY we were doing everything. It was an attempt to make Scrum a magic bullet that would automatically solve our problems for us just by using the Scrum terminology and partially adapting to the structure that Scrum requires. It was only when we stopped talking about the things and started to focus on the people that we started to have a real breakthrough. As we started introducing a new practice (actually re-introducing), we talked about why we wanted to do it and got an understanding from the team before we moved ahead. When the teams believed in what we were doing, the real transformation took place. We stopped just "doing Agile" and started to "BE Agile." Simply using new terminology on top of what was a largely existing process, with no fundamental shift in how we worked, led to dramatic failure.

Simply doing all of the things that the Scrum framework dictates is not enough. It is important that we do everything -- in fact it is required -- but we need to do it so that we can be it. Scrum gives us the skeleton upon which we can build an Agile organization. The roles, events, and artifacts of Scrum allow us to change how we operate, but we have to be willing and empowered to make that change. The underlying change in how we approach our work is what truly makes us Agile, regardless of the framework. Scrum demands that we ask the hard questions of ourselves and others, and make important decisions based upon what we learn. We understand that the team is the fundamental unit, and that we require all of the individuals in their specific roles for the team to succeed. It recognizes that we succeed and fail as a team, and that it is okay to fail, because that leads to opportunities for additional growth. We are able to push outside of our comfort zones and undertake new challenges with safety. There is room for experimentation.

All of these factors work together, within the structural guidelines of the Scrum Framework, to drive us ahead to new territory. It is our willingness to embrace the chaos that comes with change, and to fearlessly examine both how we work and the work itself, that creates opportunities for growth, both as individuals and as a team. It is when we do all of these things that we move from just "doing Scrum" and into truly "being Agile."

Our Team

We will be working throughout this book with a Scrum Team, and checking in periodically to see how we can apply various tools and techniques. Team PAWS is working on a custom mobile application to monitor your pet while you are away and a pet sitter is checking in to make sure your pet is happy in your absence. The application is brand new and the team is very excited to be developing this. They are all pet owners who like to go away on vacation sometimes and would benefit from the very app they are developing!

The Scrum Team consists of the following people:

Developers: Roger, Pradip, Stacey, Christine, Marten
Product Owner: Sarah
Scrum Master: James

The team of Developers for Team PAWS is brand new. All of them have been with the company prior to forming this team but have never worked together as a unit before forming Team PAWS. When the product was announced, they all wanted in and are feeling empowered. The team's manager, Tim, is not part of the team of Developers, but he is dedicated to seeing Team PAWS succeed. The team of Developers is completely cross-functional, although members have deep expertise in certain areas: Roger is considered an expert on mobile architecture; Pradip is a database specialist; Stacey is a UX designer; Christine is adept at creating high-performance middleware; and Marten is an experienced Quality Engineer, specializing in testing and automation. Note that QE is considered an integral part of the Developers and not a separate function or shared service!

Sarah is an experienced Product Owner but new to the organization. She has very specific ideas on how Scrum should work from her previous job and would like to see them applied here when working with Team PAWS. She has a clear vision for the application and has laid out a roadmap for what the product will do going forward. She knows what needs to be in version 1.0 and has strong ideas concerning future releases. Sarah has some experience with Story Mapping and tightly manages her Product Backlog to keep it up to date in real time.

James has been a Scrum Master with the company for 10 years but has never worked with any of the members of Team PAWS before. He is extremely passionate about Scrum and has been entrusted by the organization to drive change to make the Team PAWS product a success. He loves what he does for work and comes in bursting with energy and enthusiasm every day. He is an expert listener and a willing coach.

II - A Tale of Three Transformations

Scrum-pster Fire

Agile Transformation is hard. It takes commitment from the entire organization and a long-term plan for how to get there. Getting everyone to Agile isn't just a matter of flipping a switch and making it happen. It can take years to get there.

Makes sense, right?
You would think.

This is not a case study or a scenario I made up to illustrate a point. This is a real-world tale about watching a failure happen before my eyes and the impact it had upon the company. The name of the company and any individuals involved have been eliminated, but everything that happened is essentially as described. (Some things have been omitted for the sake of relative brevity.) Those of you who know me and have worked alongside me may recognize what follows.

Want to make sure your Agile transformation succeeds? Take heed of the many mistakes herein.

In the beginning, this was a 100% waterfall shop. Not a line of code was written without a detailed requirements document, which was frozen before development started. Nothing was tested until it was completely coded. Spending large amounts of time doing nothing but bug fixing prior to a release was not uncommon. Why?

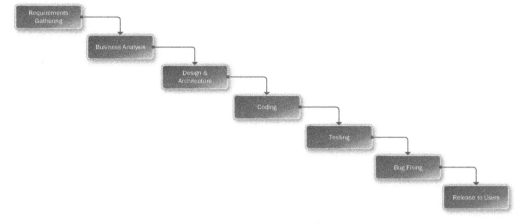

Figure 1 - Waterfall required everything to happen sequentially

"That I can tell you in one word: Tradition! (Tradition, tradition... tradition!)" Yes, it was as shaky as a fiddler on the roof.

Then one morning everything changed. That morning, the Developers were summoned into the conference room. The VP of Software Development told us "We are an Agile shop now" and gave a basic Death by PowerPoint overview of how Scrum works. There was no information on why we were doing any of this, of course. We were simply told that this was how we were working now, and that was it. We were now a Scrum Team of approximately 20 people, and the VP was the Scrum Master. There was no coaching. There was no servant-leadership. It was a textbook example of "What is thy bidding, my Scrum Master?"

The Product Backlog was a spreadsheet that he maintained. Oh, did I neglect to mention that he was also the Product Owner? He didn't say that... but he was. There was never a Sprint Backlog. We worked completely off the Product Backlog and he guarded it rigorously. The items in the Product Backlog were not user stories – they were barely Product Backlog Items (PBIs) – they were line items from a larger requirements document. Yes, the BRD was still very much a thing that we were working from.

The only ceremony that was regularly held was the Daily Scrum. We were told there were three questions that we had to answer every morning:

- What did I work on yesterday, and how long did each task take me?
- What am I working on today, and how long do I think each task will take?
- Do I have any blockers?

As you answered the first question, he would add up the hours, and if you came in anywhere less than eight, you got the added bonus of, "That isn't a full day's work. What else did you do?" If you took longer to do something than he had estimated in the master spreadsheet, or didn't finish something, you would be held accountable immediately for the missing time. This also applied for the second question. There needed to be eight hours of work or you were clearly slacking. 100% utilization was required at all times, and there was no room for any deviation. To make things that much more interesting, the team did very little of the estimating. Estimates were often provided from top level management based on how many hours they thought it should take. The person who did the actual work was then held to that estimate.

Impediments were not addressed in a meaningful way by the VP Scrum Master. His method of removing an impediment was to tell the developer to "Call that person on the phone after this meeting."

Work was routinely assigned by the VP (or one of his designees) to individuals. Because there was no actual Sprint Backlog, the team was expected to just do absolutely everything. There was no commitment. There was no feeling by the Developers that they were in any way in control.

The Daily Scrum – timeboxed to 15 minutes – would routinely take 45 minutes to an hour as 20 people gave a detailed status report.

Nobody walked out of a Daily Scrum feeling empowered.

Sprint Planning? Nope. The VP used the estimates in his spreadsheet and decided what we would work on that Sprint, based on a fully loaded 80 hours. He would have a border line on the worksheet to indicate what he expected to be completed.   Work items were routinely carried over, because it was literally impossible to complete everything during a single Sprint. We didn't plan, we just kept working down the never-ending spreadsheet that was planned for us. Sprints were routinely extended by a week or more. To make it worse, a Sprint that was extended would often be extended again. Timeboxing meant nothing.

QE was invariably running a Sprint behind, if not more, because coding was happening right up until the final hour, if not beyond.

The Sprint Review? That didn't ever actually happen. There would be the occasional demo, but that's as far as it went. Stakeholders never saw working software until it was released, and releases were few and far between.

Sprint Retrospectives? We held those about half the time. They weren't meaningful in any way. We would go around the table and talk about what we did well and what we didn't do well. The first person who spoke would have something useful to say, and there was a lot of "+1 on that for me" as we went around the table. The VP spoke last and used the Sprint Retrospective as a forum to tell the team how we messed up. For everything the team felt they did well, he would often have two things that he felt were just horribly wrong in his opinion, and he would take advantage of the captive audience to harangue the team. We were often told how another team was doing so much better than we were and there was no excuse for failure. There were no action items identified. There was no opportunity to inspect and adapt.

Nobody walked out of a Sprint Retrospective feeling empowered.

In addition, there were routine defect triage meetings. Every single defect that was logged would be reviewed, discussed in detail, and the person assigned to that defect would be asked about the status and when it could be resolved. This was separate from the Daily Scrum, and team members were responsible for both. These meetings could easily take up to two hours.

Nobody wanted to attend the triage meeting, and absolutely nobody walked out of one feeling empowered.

The mindset of the Developers became "Cover Your Ass." Because estimates were all in hours, padding your estimates became automatic just to protect yourself. If asked why your estimate was so high, it became routine to make up some nonsense about not being familiar with the code, not able to reproduce a defect, or just that there could be downstream effects that you need to make sure you took into account. The padded hours became a way to account for time that you couldn't otherwise account for - just burn off an extra hour here and there and it would balance out. There were separate estimates for development and for testing, not a single vision of the entire work. Software and Quality Engineers seemed to be viewed not as professionals, but as mere code monkeys, any of whom could easily be replaced.

The VP definitely had favorites, and he protected them. He also had people whom he regularly singled out as being problems. Those people could do the most amazing work in the world, but they would be expected to do more, and the smallest defect became a showstopper.

It wasn't safe to fail. Failure meant you were bad. Period. There was no room to experiment. There was no time allocated for that -- you had to stay on task and within your estimates.

There were no unit tests. There was no time for that. Automated unit test code was considered time wasted. All testing happened in QE, and they were responsible for their own sets of hourly estimates on each item in the spreadsheet.

There was no build automation. A full build took an entire day, and there was no QE work until a build had been completed. Obviously, it follows that Quality Engineers spent long periods of time with little to do, followed by days – if not weeks – of being completely buried when all the development work hit them at once.

Morale was the lowest I have ever seen, anywhere. There were routine lockouts on taking time off, and it wasn't the company's fault that you couldn't carry it all over from year to year. People stuck around because we truly enjoyed working together, or in some cases simply because they needed a job. Everyone wanted to do great things, but felt like it was impossible. Everyone knew waterfall was awful, but everyone would have gone back to it in a second given the chance. Getting up and going to work in the morning was hard.

Obviously, reading this it's clear that the company was not doing Scrum. This was a highly bastardized form of Scrum -- using the Scrum terminology, mixed with a lot of waterfall, and even more micromanagement -- all in the hands of someone who needed to be in total control of everything. The mistakes above are so numerous that were I to get into detail on each one it would take this entire book. You could make the case that I do exactly that, actually. There are a few, however, that are so egregious they must be touched on while in context:

- You can't simply become Agile by saying "We are Agile." That's the equivalent of your child telling you "I'm a monster" and making growling sounds at you. It's amusing, and it gets annoying after a while, but nothing has actually changed.
- There is NO place for the evil "how long did this take you" question, or any inference of it. Not in the Daily Scrum; not anywhere. Hours are not actually important. Tracking time for accounting purposes is different and has nothing to do with Scrum.
- Everyone was forced to be at 100% utilization, 100% of the time. There was no time for anything else that helps make a team awesome, let alone any kind of team building. Self-preservation was the goal every single day.
- Every Sprint should have a Goal, and everything done in the Sprint should be working toward that goal! Without a goal, the Developers are just doing stuff.

- A 20-person team of Developers is at least two times larger than it should be. We should be aiming for Teams of 3-9 people, with a number somewhere in the middle likely being the sweet spot.
- The Developers own their work and self-organize to get it done. The work is not assigned by upper management to a particular developer, and the Developers work with the Product Owner to determine what work they are going to take on during a Sprint in order to deliver the maximum value. This isn't an endless list of work that is unmanageable!
- Repeating the above: the Developers own their work. This includes design, architecture and QE. Everyone is responsible for getting Product Backlog Items to Done.
- Sprint Retrospectives should never be about berating the team for everything they did wrong! This is the most powerful opportunity the team has to identify ways they can be even more awesome.
- Bugs and Product Backlog Items were tracked completely separately. There were, in effect, two different Product Backlogs. The two would overlap from time to time, but not always.
- The focus was not on people, but on process. By doing this, the people all felt completely disenfranchised and not empowered. The old command-and-control structure still held sway.

Rebel Sc(r)um

So here we are in the throes of a soul-killing transformation to Scrum that actually wasn't one. The general feeling amongst the Developers was to throw Scrum/Agile out as a total disaster and go back to what we were doing. Even when we knew that waterfall was evil, it was at least kind of functioning, and we were putting out working software sometimes.

But there were rebels.

Rebels who were familiar with how Scrum is supposed to work, or who spent some time with Google and learned that something was terribly, terribly wrong. Many a blog was read, many a book was purchased and consumed. And a plan was devised.

Before I lay out this nefarious scheme, a caveat. I don't actually recommend this plan. It worked for this group, but we got lucky. And yes, I was most certainly one of the aforementioned rebels. While we were sure it would work – and ultimately it did – it could just have easily exploded in our faces.

In order for our wicked plot to succeed, there first needed to be a critical sea change at the top of the management chain. A new executive joined the company and brought new energy along with him. This forced the oft-mentioned VP to back off, and paved the way for change. (The VP was, in fairly rapid order, no longer with the company). A true Agile transformation needs buy-in vertically throughout the organization. It's not necessarily top-down, but top-level management has to be on board.

We didn't actually do that - instead deciding that we would rather ask for forgiveness than permission, so we acted. Scrum was poison, so we had to spin it and take a different approach. How to get the team to embrace Scrum without ever telling them what they were doing? Almost every term associated with Scrum was out. We needed to be stealthy and get everyone on board with the idea of just being awesome again and willing to try things. But this time, rather than coming from a VP with a decree, it was coming from two or three peers who just wanted us to be great and have fun doing it.

We recognized that the one ceremony people felt was at least sort of useful was the Daily Scrum. Our first step was to just call it a stand-up (which is not uncommon, but more on that later) and to change how it was run. Hours were obviously gone. We moved to an actual board, and we suggested that we change the conversation to a story-by-story basis, rather than focusing on individuals. This took the pressure off people and refocused the conversation on the work and how things were progressing. I became the Scrum Master, but to the team I was just the guy facilitating the meeting. There was to be no mention of the word "Scrum."

The 20-person team was divided into manageable sizes. Some of this was done by management (definitely a Scrum anti-pattern), but for now we were fine with this compromise. The teams weren't in a place to self-organize at that level yet anyway.

Sprint Retrospectives had to be completely overhauled. For a long time, we didn't do them. When we noticed that the teams were starting to talk about how to improve, we jumped. We started "discussion meetings" at the end of every Sprint before we did any planning. We stopped just going around a table and asking people what they thought, and started to make things more open-ended, giving team members a chance to have a discussion, and asking thoughtful, leading questions to steer the discussion toward arriving at SMART goals for how to adapt going forward.

Sprint Planning became a real thing, and the team became engaged and involved with the work they would be doing. To begin with, estimates were out the window, because we wanted to break the habit of trying to break down everything into hours. We simply asked the question "What do think the team can complete during this Sprint?" and built the backlog accordingly. Burndown and Burnup charts weren't important. All that mattered was that the team agreed on what they could do, and that they got it done.

At the same time, we started to preach two important things to the teams:
1. It's okay to fail.
2. It's better to under-commit and over-deliver than the reverse.

We did shorten to one-week Sprints for a long time, to help establish cadence and the discipline of limiting work to what could be realized during the Sprint. The accelerated pace of using one-week Sprints proved to be critical for our teams. It increased focus and kept the amount of work in progress to a minimum, as we focused on getting to Done.

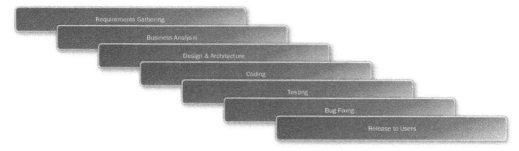

Figure 2 - Scrum creates overlapping and continuous work

The energy began to change, and the teams were feeling like they could do anything. Everyone was talking instead of building silos and sulking. People were excited about what they were accomplishing, no matter how difficult the work. We were learning together and helping each other along the way. If you fell, there was someone there to pick you up and help out. Engineers were sitting two or three in a room, collaborating on the same Product Backlog Item. The basic "Cover Your Ass" mentality stopped, and the teams began thinking of themselves as teams! This was the breakthrough we were waiting for!

Somewhere around here... we let the cat out of the bag. The teams were (mostly) doing Scrum. We just weren't calling it that. But this was now a good time to start using the right language, and to look how far we had come as a group!

We might have been called sneaky bastards. We might have high-fived immediately after that.

Somewhere during this process, we introduced CI/CD builds. We introduced nightly full staging builds for QE. We started writing automated unit tests and showing them to everyone like we had just made a new discovery. Not everyone bought into unit tests right away, but they saw how they could be awesome. (We also got our asses chewed out by a boss-type for bringing unit tests into the picture without asking him first. Forgiveness, not permission, right?) We got people thinking about how to refactor code, and how spending time writing clean code up front was better than writing something quickly and ending up

15

with a code base more fragile than a house of cards. Tech Debt started to slowly get paid down, and engineering practices leveled up! We created a wall that just held sticky notes of known Tech Debt, so everyone was aware of areas that required attention, and we had the freedom to act on paying that down at any time when we had free cycles.

All that said - this was not easy! There was a lot of work that went into making these changes, and it had to be done with care. We were met with resistance on many levels. We were challenged on almost everything. Some people just didn't get it, others didn't see the value in what we were trying, others probably saw through our thinly disguised charade and declared there were shenanigans. You know what? All of those people who resisted were right to do so! We barely had permission to do what we were doing, and the approach we took flew in the face of any so-called conventional wisdom. There were many days when we were just making it up and seeing if it worked, and sometimes it showed. But we eventually got there and created high-performing Scrum Teams out of actual chaos.

We recognized the chaos we were left with, came up with a plan, and worked slowly and calmly to create something awesome out of that initial chaos. Use the energy that tumultuousness brings to create your own awesome!

Applied knowledge

When we last left our intrepid group of rebels, they (okay, we) had turned an initial Agile Transformation attempt that was an utter failure into successful first steps at actually implementing Scrum. And it was good. The teams were happy, collaborative, and productive. The walls were coming down and things were proceeding nicely.

And then things began to change again.

As before, it started from above. We had another change in our management team, and with it a new approach. She loved what we were doing and wanted to see us expand on that and be even more amazing.

16

What's more, she wanted to SCALE to the entire development organization. We were not prepared.

We began to hear rumblings that changes were afoot. There would be training. There could be coaching. Once again, a select few of us sat back and smiled and quietly high-fived when we thought nobody was watching (and sometimes when we knew they were). This was actual progress. We started hearing words like "alignment" thrown around like we meant them.

Enter an actual professional Agile Coach.

Over a two-week period, we were involved in intensive training, and hands-on planning across teams, identifying dependencies between teams, working from a common Product Backlog, and learning techniques to help identify value and become better at estimating. We started really thinking about Capacity vs. Load vs. Velocity and recognizing the differences between these three things. Roles were shifted and re-defined. I relinquished my role as Scrum Master to others and put on the hat of an in-house Agile Coach (not the actual title, but close enough here).

The teams suffered. This was predictable. We had shaken things up a lot and time was required to make the necessary adjustments. Within two Sprints, everything changed.

Every two weeks, in the middle of the Sprint(s), we would have a check-in call to keep upper management up to date as to how the products were doing, and to raise impediments to the management team that the Scrum Teams were not able to resolve on their own. For the first couple of calls, there was remarkable parity on how all teams were performing. By about the third Sprint for the teams I worked with (and we were two Sprints behind other teams from an alignment perspective), we started to notice that the Developers we had already started transforming just took off. They were producing extremely high-quality work. The defect rate was way down. They were exceeding their expected velocity - and not by a small amount. There was rejoicing.

While this was happening, the other teams in the organization were struggling. This didn't make sense to them. The cries to abandon Scrum and just go back to what they were doing were growing. When these same teams suddenly saw our team's explosion in quality and productivity, these voices of dissent turned into voices of curiosity. What were we doing that they weren't? How can they get to the same point?

The answer, of course, was that they just needed time and more active coaching to help them through the struggles they were facing. We had highly-collaborative highly-performing teams because we had already fostered and nurtured that environment, and once we got used to the shift in how we were looking at work, the rest came naturally.

But we had a real-world example -- what we were all trained on worked. We were able to answer questions from the other teams, provide guidance, and talk about what we did to get through the exact same issues they were facing. One by one, we could see the lights go on, and teams hit their stride.

At this point, let me back up a little. Remember the beginning of this journey? The abject failure that was the initial Agile Transformation? Let's go back there briefly and start bringing things full-circle.

During that initial Agile-Because-I-Say-So attempt, the team (one enormous team, remember) was told frequently that the teams working on other products were succeeding and outperforming us, and we were the proverbial red-headed stepchild in the organization because this wasn't working for us. So, when we moved from Micromanagement-As-Agile into actually doing Scrum, it was even more disruptive to these teams. They had been told they were doing Scrum and it was working, and the training was contrary to absolutely everything they knew. Scrum may be disruptive, but this became an extreme example.

We saw valuable team members leave, and the fear of failure was real. We saw people who sort of understood it, step up and do their best to right the ship. I was on Skype calls daily talking to people; answering questions, providing coaching, or just being a willing ear when they needed to talk to someone and get it off their chest. What I heard, almost universally, was that when they saw how it was working for other teams, they used that as motivation. They knew they could get there.

It took time, as previously indicated. Having an environment where the teams who were struggling with change could feel safe when they failed, and could see that Scrum was successful, provided the reassurance to get through the struggle. When everything clicked, and those teams saw the same results, the celebration was tremendous.

This journey was arduous. It took forever, and a lot of sneaking around how we were doing things. Ultimately, what made it work was a willingness to try anything and a willingness to fail. If something didn't work, we had no problem trying something else until we found what did work. We got there, with many lessons learned along the way.

III - Bringing the Scrum Values to Life

Why the Scrum Values are Important

One of the best things that happened to the Scrum Guide in the last few years was the introduction of the Scrum Values. These two very simple paragraphs shine a huge light on things that are crucial to the success of Scrum. I've spent a lot of time thinking about each one, how they impact what we do each day, and want to look at each one in turn.

- Commitment
- Courage
- Focus
- Openness
- Respect

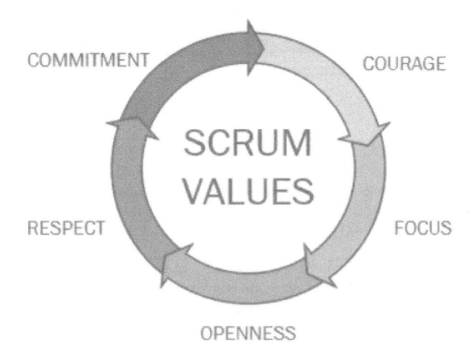

SCRUM VALUES

COMMITMENT

COURAGE

RESPECT

FOCUS

OPENNESS

Figure 3 - The Scrum Values work together seamlessly

Quoting from the November 2020 Scrum Guide:

Successful use of Scrum depends on people becoming more proficient in living five values:

Commitment, Focus, Openness, Respect, and Courage

The Scrum Team commits to achieving its goals and to supporting each other. Their primary focus is on the work of the Sprint to make the best possible progress toward these goals. The Scrum Team and its stakeholders are open about the work and the challenges. Scrum Team members respect each other to be capable, independent people, and are respected as such by the people with whom they work. The Scrum Team members have the courage to do the right thing, to work on tough problems.

21

These values give direction to the Scrum Team with regard to their work, actions, and behavior. The decisions that are made, the steps taken, and the way Scrum is used should reinforce these values, not diminish or undermine them. The Scrum Team members learn and explore the values as they work with the Scrum events and artifacts. When these values are embodied by the Scrum Team and the people they work with, the empirical Scrum pillars of transparency, inspection, and adaptation come to life building trust.

Two paragraphs and change. Lots of information to digest. Each one of these Scrum Values is so important. These aren't just words that we can consider and forget, they are imperative to how we create highly collaborative, highly productive teams.

It is worth pointing out right here that I actually wrote this part after I drafted everything that follows. One of the best parts of examining each of the Scrum Values, to me, was examining how each one relates very strongly to the others. Considering each individually, it becomes clear how all five are tightly connected and provide crucial pillars upon which Scrum is built.

Commitment

That's a huge word that carries a lot of weight. Commitment can be scary. It's also a word that has had a shift in definition (as it relates to Scrum) in recent times. So, what exactly do we mean when we are talking about commitment?

For a long time, commitment meant "I am going to do everything it takes -- working nine days a week, 27.5 hours a day, if necessary -- to make sure this gets done exactly on time and exactly as described by the requirements." For some people, this is still what it means -- being on call non-stop, never being able to disconnect, even on vacation, and putting that commitment above all else. In a traditional waterfall command-and-control structure this is still how people view the word commitment.

That's not how this works. That's not how any of this works.

Go back to the Scrum Guide for a minute. Got it? Now search for the word "commitment" in there. As of the November 2020 update there is exactly one place you will find it, and that's in the Scrum Values. Further, the Scrum Guide states: "The Scrum Team commits to achieving its goals and to supporting each other. "[ii] That's it.

Commitment doesn't mean we have no life and pull out every single last stop to get everything done exactly as commanded by some arcane (and likely out of date) requirements document. In fact, if a superhero effort is required by one or more members of the team to accomplish their Sprint Goal, it's actually an important indicator that something is not working correctly.

- Commitment means that everyone on the team is dedicated to helping the team succeed. The exact work that will be done within a Sprint can and will change as work is underway, but always with the end desire of achieving the Sprint Goals.
- Commitment means that if we are behind, the Developers will sit with the Product Owner and have a conversation to make adjustments to the work in the Sprint so that an increment of working software is done when the Sprint ends.
- Commitment means that the Product Owner leaves flexibility in his or her Acceptance Criteria so that the team has room for negotiation.
- Commitment means that the Scrum Master is actively listening and responding to the needs of the team.
- Commitment means that we are going to do our best, but recognize that if we fall short it will not be for lack of effort.
- Commitment means that we are committed to each other and willing to help out when a fellow team member is stuck or blocked in any way.

Organizationally, commitment means that we empower our Scrum Teams and give them the resources and flexibility they need to be successful. Management becomes leadership. We are actively clearing the way for our teams and allowing them the freedom to succeed without daily control. It means we have created an environment in which it is safe to experiment and safe to fail -- as long as we are always moving forward.

When the Developers set their Sprint Backlog, we should stop talking about commitment – as it relates to the old way of thinking – and recognize that we are talking about a forecast. Things may change as we get more clarity on any or all user stories in a Sprint. Things may be moved out, or be added, to allow the team to still meet the Sprint Goal.

That doesn't mean the team failed to meet its commitments, it means they are being truly Agile.

Courage

Courage is an easy thing to understand. It's also incredibly hard for people to fully embrace when we are dealing with the Scrum Values. As before, I want to start by looking at the one sentence in the Scrum Guide that applies:

"The Scrum Team members have courage to do the right thing, to work on tough problems."
iii

There is it in a nutshell. Do the right thing and work on tough problems. There's a whole lot more below the surface of that sentence though.

When we talk about team members doing the right thing, there is an implied "even when it's hard" at the end:
- Courage means not reverting to old habits when work is challenging.
- Courage means not taking shortcuts and getting work done quickly simply for the sake of getting it done quickly.
- Courage means asking difficult questions when we don't have all of the information we need to build a product.
- Courage means adapting to change.
- Courage means trusting the entire Scrum Team.
- Courage means doing everything in our power to meet our forecast and stick to the Definition of Done.

- Courage means committing.
- Courage means being honest about our work.
- Courage means listening to what others on our team are saying, even when we don't want to hear it.
- Courage means asking for help when we are stuck and accepting help when it is offered to us.
- Courage means failing and having the courage to admit it.

Some of the biggest issues I have seen with teams who are struggling with Scrum come down to courage. It's very easy to fall back into familiar patterns and even easier to point fingers when things don't work.

The ceremonies of the Daily Scrum, Sprint Planning, Sprint Review, and Retrospective all require courage. For Scrum to succeed, we must be able to talk about things that aren't going well and come up with ways to fix them. We have to be willing to show the cracks in our armor to the team and trust that the team will help us to overcome obstacles.

Showing work in the Sprint Review takes a huge amount of courage. We accept that we might get feedback that we may not like, and we go into the meeting only prepared to show work that has met our Definition of Done. We are not going to show our stakeholders (and each other) work that is half-finished, and we are not going to hand-wave past the incomplete parts. We also aren't going to show stakeholders a chunk of code they don't necessarily understand; we will only show them work as our users will see it. Our stakeholders might not be technical, and it's likely they are not interested in our architecture, our code, or how and why something works. They want to see our product as our users will experience it and provide honest feedback based on work that has been completed.

We are willing to have an honest discussion every day to inspect our progress toward our Sprint Goals and adapt our plan if we are off track. We have a cross-functional team that is willing to jump into work they may know little about and get it done as a team. We are willing to be honest in our Retrospectives and discuss ways we can be a better team. We do this without throwing our teammates under the bus, but instead are willing

25

to share in our failures as much as we are willing to celebrate our successes.

Scrum takes a tremendous amount of personal and team courage. The courage demanded by Scrum allows us to shine a bright light on every aspect of what we do in order to look at it clearly and always find ways to make improvements.

Focus

Once again, from the Scrum Guide:

"Their primary focus is on the work of the Sprint to make the best possible progress toward these goals."[iv]

In the section about commitment, I touched on the importance of setting our forecast for the Sprint in accordance with the Sprint Goals. In the section about courage, the importance of adhering to our Definition of Done made an appearance. These things have something else in common. To make both of these things happen, we need Focus.

In some ways, Focus is perhaps the simplest of the Sprint Values for us to consider. In other ways, it is much more complicated.

The easiest way to think about Focus is to look within the context of a Sprint. During Sprint Planning the Developers work with the Product Owner and select what they will be working on within that Sprint. In order to meet that forecast, the Developers must focus solely on the selected work.

- The team does not work on anything that is outside of the Sprint Goal.
- The team does not work on anything that does not provide value to the Increment.
- If someone makes a new request of the Developers, direct the requestor to the Product Owner.

- When there is something that is preventing the team from making progress, bring it to the attention of the Scrum Master and resume work toward the Sprint Goal.

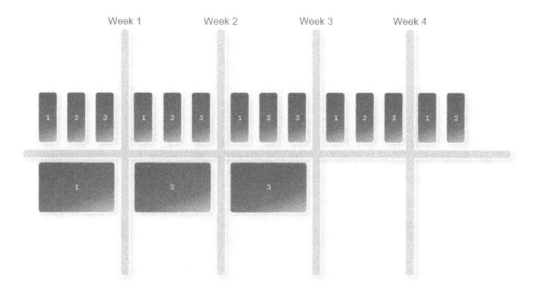

Figure 4 - Focusing on one thing at a time helps the Developers finish work faster

Going beyond just that, it's easy to see other ways in which Focus is an important part of how Scrum makes us more effective! One of the most effective ways to get a User Story done is to swarm on that item. When the team swarms on the one or two most valuable/important things in the Sprint Backlog and gets each to Done before moving on, the team's velocity skyrockets. When we are focused on those one or two things, it's much easier to spot the trouble areas and come up with a plan to deal with uncertainty. Focus is what allows us to make sure all of our important ceremonies in Scrum fit within their timeboxes. We aren't having meetings purely for the sake of having meetings, but we are concentrating on the task at hand.

Distilled into its simplest form, focus gets us to Done and lets us become faster and more productive.

Openness

Now that we have the first three values established, we move into the two that really start to pull everything together into a whole. We start here with Openness. Once more, from the Scrum Guide:

"The Scrum Team and its stakeholders are open about the work and the challenges. "[v]

It's pretty amazing how one sentence summarizes it all. Scrum demands that we be completely open about everything we are doing. Period. There are no secrets. There is no building of silos and obfuscating work to hide what we are doing. Instead, we want to make everything known to everyone -- starting with ourselves!

- Openness means we talk about our progress toward the Sprint Goal every day.
- Openness means we talk about where we are falling short and enter into discussion on how to get back on track.
- Openness means that when we aren't on track, we don't offer excuses or try to hand-wave our way past an issue.
- Openness means we put all our work on the Scrum Board so anyone can see what we are working on and our progress toward Done.
- Openness means everyone is welcome into any of our Scrum ceremonies to learn more about our progress and what our product looks like.
- Openness means we are willing to keep the Product Owner up to date as work moves toward Done so he/she can accept that work in real time.
- Openness means we are willing to raise impediments to the Scrum Master so he/she can remove them and let the team focus.
- Openness means we are willing to have the difficult conversations and trust each other to help the entire team succeed.

Your Jedi mind tricks don't work in Scrum. In fact, they will backfire. We don't like to talk about our shortfalls, as individuals or as a team, but when we try to mask them or ignore them, we actively damage the team.

Being open about our progress toward the Sprint Goal requires Commitment.
Being open about where we are struggling requires Courage.
Being open about the most important things we are working on requires Focus.

The Agile Manifesto explicitly tells us the importance of Openness right away. We value individuals and interactions over processes and tools. We recognize that sitting down and talking to people, openly and honestly, is the best way to convey information.

Openness pulls things together and allows the team to honestly inspect our progress and make adaptations as required to stay on track. When that openness is compromised, the rest of our Sprint Values are compromised with it.

Respect

And here we get to the heart of everything. Respect. One last time, the Scrum Guide:
"Scrum Team members respect each other to be capable, independent people, and are respected as such by the people with whom they work."[vi]

I've seen what can happen when respect is lost, and it's not pretty, my friends.

Have you sat in a team meeting or event (pick one, any one) where one person talks over the rest of the team? Had someone who simply will not listen to any opinion other than his or her own? How about the meeting where one or more members of the Developers refuses to listen to the Product Owner or Scrum Master because he/she "knows better" or "has been doing this longer than you have"? Have you seen a team lead who tells the rest of the team to do what he says rather than let them self-manage work or swarm on the most valuable items in the Sprint Backlog? Have you had the team member who brings his/her laptop into a Retrospective or Sprint Planning meeting and is too busy sending emails to pay attention to what is happening in the room?

Better yet, have you seen all of those in the same person?
I have, and it's horrible.

How about the Product Owner or Scrum Master who intentionally moves to sit near the door so he can monitor when everyone enters and leaves, and keeps track of exactly how long each person is away from their desk because they demand 100% utilization? Have you thrown your hands up in exasperation at the end of a meeting, or at the end of a day, and wanted to just scream because it feels like you could have spent your time better poking knitting needles through your arms?

Those things are fun too!

In fact, I don't even have to think that hard to come up with an example of each of these disrespectful behaviors. Look back at the first chapter. The lack of respect for the team is all over that, and everyone on that team – myself included – felt it. Want to take a great team and make them completely dysfunctional? Stop showing them any kind of respect and see what happens.

Without respect, the rest of the Scrum Values are just words. They mean nothing. We can't do anything else if we don't show ourselves and everyone on our Scrum Teams respect:

- Respect means actively listening when someone else is talking, even if we don't really want to hear what they are saying. Especially then.
- Respect means firmly believing that every person on our team is awesome and can do any task they put their minds to.
- Respect means knowing that every member of our Scrum Team is absolutely professional, is dedicated to doing their best at all times, and wants the entire team to succeed.

- Respect means understanding that the entire room is smarter than the smartest person in the room, and valuing what the entire team has to say.
- Respect means valuing the input of our stakeholders — who want the best possible product for all our users — both internal and external.
- Respect means recognizing the importance of being on time for meetings and staying within timeboxes.
- Respect means respecting our process.

When we lose respect, the team suffers.
- We lack Commitment because we start becoming too busy looking out for ourselves and not the team.
- We lack Courage because we have already accepted defeat.
- We lack Focus because our minds are preoccupied or we allow ourselves to be distracted.
- We lack Openness because we cannot trust.

When we lack a team mentality, we devolve into a group of individuals who might happen to be working on similar things but in a manner that is completely self-contained. Our velocity suffers. Our quality suffers. Our happiness suffers. Our product suffers. Our company suffers.

Respect is the foundation upon which all of the other Scrum Values rest. A lack of respect by any member of the team is something that simply cannot be allowed. It must be addressed quickly, or the damage will be swift and lasting.

Lead by example. Show every member of your team absolute respect during all of your interactions with them. Truly listen to everything they are telling you and ask questions to understand when you are not sure of something. Value their input because they probably have information you don't. Recognize that without each member of the team, dedicated to doing a great job for the team, the entire team would fail.

Respect breeds respect. Give a lot, and you will get a lot. Withhold it, and you will never get it. Without respect at its deepest level, a team will never be successful, no matter what else you do.

IV - Scrum at Me, Bro!

"Scrum is hard and disruptive" -- Ken Schwaber

The Scrum Guide is deceptively short. Don't make the mistake of thinking that the brevity makes it something that is simple to do; it is not. The Scrum Guide provides us with a framework upon which we build to create highly performing, highly adaptive, and highly collaborative teams. Scrum is not going to solve your problems, but it is going to make them obvious and provide you with the means with which to make important changes in the way you work. It requires a great deal of effort and attention to detail to succeed. This is not a prescriptive "set and forget" methodology. In fact, it is not a methodology at all.

Scrum is intentionally simple to understand and difficult to master. We have to fundamentally shift how we work, and that change can be extremely challenging. When we implement Scrum, we shift from focusing on outputs to outcomes, we change from looking at what is releasable to what is valuable. There is only ONE definition of Scrum (www.scrumguides.org), but there is no single way to implement it. There are no absolute truths, solutions, or best practices in Scrum -- those are up to your organization and way of working. Scrum provides us with a way to constantly check ourselves and our products against reality, to re-align and make constant adaptations as we gain new insights.

Empirically Speaking

Scrum is built on empiricism. Simply put, that means that we are gaining knowledge from our actual experience and making decisions based on what we know. We aren't making things up as we go, but as a team we are applying our knowledge to continually make improvements in how we work.

The traditional waterfall methodology is predictive. We take a lot of time to try to figure out absolutely everything ahead of time, we write down a plan and then execute exactly that plan. We make assumptions and predictions about where technology, the market, and our business will be

— often months in advance — and hope we guessed correctly. The problem, of course, is that we always predict incorrectly, and the price that we pay at the end of the development cycle for those incorrect predictions is often quite heavy.

One of the problems we face, particularly early in an Agile transformation, is that people see Sprints as mini-waterfalls in which every activity must necessarily be preceded by another. We can't write any code until we have all of the information we need in our User Stories, and testing can't happen until everything has been written and deployed. By doing this, we end up creating dead space at the beginning and end of our Sprints where Developers feel partially handcuffed and don't know what to do next. A good user story has just enough information for the Developers to begin work, and the design will emerge as discussion around the work takes place. The dialogue between the Developers and Product Owner drive development forward on a daily basis. QE specialists can get a jump on writing test cases because they know from the Daily Scrum Meeting which User Stories are in development and will therefore be coming to them first, making it easy to prioritize their work.

All of this requires excellent technical practices, including Continuous Integration and Continuous Deployment in order to succeed. If no builds are making it from development and into testing until late in a Sprint, we have forced ourselves into a waterfall pattern, no matter how Agile we say we are being. You still need to go through all of the various stages involved in creating good software, but these stages should largely overlap each other, allowing us to turn out high quality product in short periods of time.

Scrum relies on empiricism. By working in rapid cycles and basing everything we do on the knowledge we have gained, we are better able to hit our targets in a timely manner and deliver valuable products to our customers without months of waiting. We don't try to predict; we respond to change. Our ability to succeed is closely related to our ability to be open-minded and optimistic, even when things are going wrong.

For Scrum to work, we need the three pillars of empiricism to be firmly in place:

- Transparency
- Inspection
- Adaptation

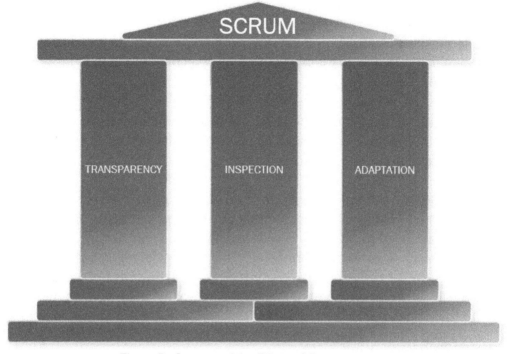

Figure 5 - Scrum and the Pillars of Empiricism

They are listed in that order for a reason. Transparency is required for Inspection to happen, and Inspection is required for Adaptation to happen. In turn, our Adaptation demands additional Transparency so that we can see the results as they happen.

Transparency

Empiricism and Scrum demand transparency. We need to be completely open about what we are doing, and how and why we are doing it. There is no place here for CYA behavior or building silos around our work. We WANT everyone to see what's going on and require that the team is always fully aware of everything surrounding their work. We are not afraid to admit mistakes or talk about areas where things aren't going quite according to plan. We state any assumptions we have made early and often, and are prepared to make adjustments should we be incorrect.

To this end, we tend to put items on boards — telling us what is Done, what is work in progress (and at what state in that process), and what hasn't been started yet. We build big visible displays to radiate information to the team and the organization. We tend to buy sticky notes and markers in bulk to keep all of our information up to date in as close to real time as possible.

Transparency means that the team is talking about their work throughout the day. It means that the team is working together on large, complex problems in order to get them to Done.

Transparency can be hard. It opens us up to exposure and criticism, and provides an opportunity for confrontation. In an organization where people are used to building up silos and hoarding knowledge, transparency is absolutely terrifying. The benefits of being truly transparent far outweigh the potential negatives, however. Confrontation is easily turned into conversation, exposure shines a light on where we are having problems, and criticism becomes constructive as we look for ways to get better.

Inspection

We don't work in a vacuum. It's important that at regular intervals we inspect both our work and the way we are working. Obviously, this demands that we have transparency into everything so that we can have this discussion and improve our understanding of our work and our processes. The Daily Scrum, Sprint Review, and Sprint Retrospective are all opportunities for us to inspect. We talk about how we are doing and get feedback in order to gain knowledge and insight.

Inspection requires Courage. It can be hard to talk about problems we are facing as a team. Inspection requires Respect. We need to have respect for each other and for our stakeholders and be willing to accept feedback that comes from a place of wanting to improve our product and our team.

Adaptation

We can always get better. Inspection helps us to identify issues -- or potential ones -- facing our team. Adaptation allows us to act on what we have found and find ways to make improvements. We need to always be looking for Kaizen (continuous improvement) for both our work and ourselves. We take feedback from our stakeholders in the Sprint Review and turn it into actionable work in future Sprints to make our product better align with their needs. We talk about our progress in the Daily Scrum and in the Sprint Retrospective and make changes based on our newly acquired and shared knowledge to better our team.

I tell my teams that we can try anything for a Sprint or two to see if it works. When something isn't working, we talk about it more and make more changes until we hit on something that does work for us. What works for one team may not work for another, and it's important that we always keep that in mind. It's clear how adaptation happens because we have both transparency and inspection happening; without them we cannot successfully adapt.

Inspection and adaptation work in a never-ending cycle; we inspect, we adapt, and we inspect again. We fearlessly make changes and experiment to find the best solution for our problems, whether it is how we are working as a team or how we are tackling work in the Sprint Backlog.

3-5-3

At its core, the Scrum framework is simple and held up by the 3-5-3 structure: 3 Roles, 5 Events, and 3 Artifacts. You need all of these elements to be doing Scrum, nothing in there is optional. Leaving out any of the parts means you are not doing Scrum. Ken Schwaber famously likened Scrum to playing chess[vii], and it's an excellent analogy.

You can't just change the rules of chess and still claim to be playing chess; there are no house rules. If I decide that the queen can jump pieces in her way to get to another piece, I have an entirely new game (and a bad one). Scrum gives you a lot of freedom in how to make it work within your organization, but you still have to follow the basic rules.

3 Roles

'Cooperation is the act of working with others and acting together to accomplish a job. Team is a partnership of unique people who bring out the very best in each other, and who know that even though they are wonderful as individuals, they are even better together. Coming together is a beginning; keeping together is progress; working together is success.' – Paulo Caroli and TC Caetano[viii]

The three roles in Scrum are the Product Owner, the Scrum Master, and the Developers. There is exactly one Product Owner and one Scrum Master for the team, and the Developers are typically a team of 3-9 cross-functional members. As a whole, this is referred to as the Scrum Team. You need all three roles to have a complete Scrum Team. One immediate thing that jumps out to people new to Scrum is "I don't see a Project Manager, Business Analyst, Team Lead, or Team Manager anywhere in here!" That is entirely correct. That doesn't mean there is no place for them in your organization, but they are not considered part of a Scrum Team. There are only three roles, and everyone on your Scrum Teams must fall into one of those three roles or they are not considered part of the Scrum Team at all.

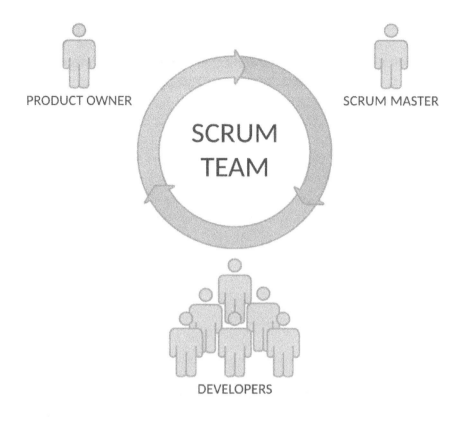

Figure 6 - The Scrum Team

Product Owner - WHAT

The Product Owner owns the Product Backlog. She is solely responsible for its upkeep and how Product Backlog Items are prioritized according to their value. Only the Product Owner can make decisions on value, and her word is final. A good PO will have a vision for the product that can be executed by the Developers. She is responsible for aligning with both the Developers and other teams to make sure the vision is attainable. The Product Owner should be always available to the team to answer questions and provide guidance into work, to look at work in progress and make sure it aligns with her vision, and to ensure that the correct value is being delivered by the team. She is also responsible for communicating with customers and stakeholders, gathering information and requirements that can be turned into future PBIs, as well as showcasing Done work for everyone to see early and often. The PO doesn't tell the Developers <u>how</u> to do the work, but trusts that they have the knowledge and expertise to make her vision a reality. Without a strong Product Owner, it becomes impossible to order the Product Backlog meaningfully, to determine what will add the most value, and to engage stakeholders to get them behind the product we are building.

The Team PAWS Product Owner, Sarah, understands all of this. She spends about half of her time talking to customers and stakeholders and the rest of the time communicating and collaborating with the others in the Scrum Team. She dedicates a portion of every Sprint to keeping her Product Backlog up to date, moving work out that will not be done soon, and making sure that everything is ordered by its value to the product as a whole. She is always available to answer questions for the Developers or to look at pieces of software as they become available to make sure the team is in alignment with her vision for the product. She is the only person responsible for her Product Backlog, and her decisions are final.

Developers - HOW
The Developers are responsible for getting the work selected in their Sprint Backlog to Done. They solely own the Sprint Backlog, and nobody can make changes to it without the team's acceptance. A great team is both self-organizing and self-managing; they decide both how they are going to work and what work they are going to do within a Sprint to maximize the value they are creating. They are able to negotiate with the PO to get the right work into a Sprint and to create a Sprint Goal. They are cross-functional – no internal team silos – and collaborative. They know best how to work together to be great. Without great Developers, the Product Owner has no way of creating a high-quality high-value product.

The Developers should have a strong T-shaped skill set; while each member may have a deep working knowledge and expertise in one or more areas, he or she possesses a wide general skill set and is considered able to work on any aspect of the product at any given time. For example, while Roger of Team PAWS is very highly specialized in mobile app architecture, he is still able to help write database code and can assist with test automation if that's what the team needs. All of the Developers have the same title – Developer – and are considered equal. There is no distinction between roles within the Developers. The team is dedicated to their product and to producing the best quality code possible. They collaborate throughout the day via pair programming, peer review, and simply talking to each other as they work through the day's challenges. Osmotic communication is second nature to the members of the Developers.

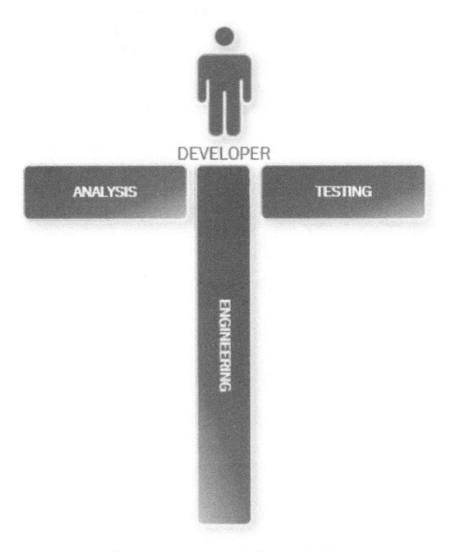

Figure 7 - An example of a T-shaped skill set

Scrum Master - PROCESS

The Scrum Master is responsible for making sure that Scrum is being followed. He is a coach, a mentor, a facilitator, and an ardent defender of the Developers. He is willing and able to aggressively remove impediments quickly. A good SM is focused on how to make his Scrum Teams the best they can possibly be, and how to drive them toward making improvements and delivering the value they have forecast. He makes work visible using information radiators of all kinds. He is creative with his approach to working with the team and is willing to try anything if it might work, as long as it still adheres to the Scrum framework. He knows that the team's success is his success and is largely external to the process of how the team functions. Without a great Scrum Master, the team has no way of knowing they are succeeding with Scrum, that impediments are being removed, and that they are finding ways to continuously improve over time.

James is an integral part of Team PAWS. He focuses on the team at all times, actively listening and participating in conversations. He looks for areas where the team is struggling and aggressively removes impediments when they arise. He understands that as the team forms, they will have a need for coaching and guidance, and he is always available to facilitate any discussion. He is willing to try anything to see if it will work for the team and isn't afraid to make mistakes as long as they help move the team forward.

5 Events

An Important Distinction
It's worth noting that all of these are Events. Sometimes they are referred to as Ceremonies. None of the Scrum Events are "meetings." One of the more common complaints is that Scrum has too many meetings, but it actually has none. Each of the events has a very distinct purpose and a fixed timebox. When you add up all of the time spent in the Scrum Events, it's actually a very small percentage of the overall Sprint. For a two-week Sprint, the total time spent in Scrum Events is under eleven hours at most and is likely to be shorter for a mature Scrum Team.

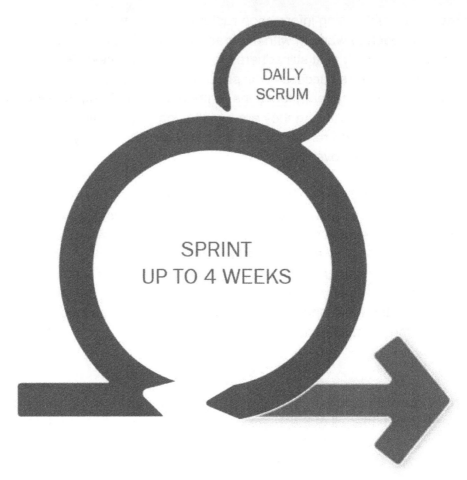

Figure 8 - The Sprint and the Daily Scrum

The Sprint

The Sprint itself is the beating heart of Scrum. This is the steady rhythm at which the Scrum Team works and in which value is created. Whether the length of the Sprint is one week or four weeks, it provides clear boundaries for the team and enables a frequent feedback loop to make sure we are delivering value to our customers on a regular basis. Every other event in Scrum depends on the Sprint itself. Sprint length can vary from team to team, depending on the product and the need to quickly inspect and adapt. The Product Owner's willingness to accept risk, in alignment with the organization, will help determine the ideal Sprint length.

Without the Sprint there is no cadence to work being delivered, there is no feedback loop allowing the team to make changes, and there is no rapid release of high-quality product.

Sprint Planning
Sprint Planning is where the Developers work with the Product Owner to take on high-value work to create a new Increment. This is the chance to not only decide what to work on, but to come up with a plan for how to get that work done. Without Sprint Planning, there is no good way to formally agree on what work will be done and how to do it. Sprint Planning will be covered in more detail later in this book.

Daily Scrum
The Daily Scrum is how the team gets together once per day for no more than 15 minutes to talk about what work has been done and to plan the next 24 hours. The Daily Scrum meeting -- though often called a Daily Standup -- does not require the team to be standing (though it is often considered a good practice for co-located teams). It's also not a status report from the Developers. Team members should be talking to each other and planning their work, not reporting to the Scrum Master and/or Product Owner to show progress toward a goal. In fact, it is not even necessary for the SM or PO to attend the Daily Scrum (though I do encourage it, in case questions arise). Just as the Sprint itself provides a rapid feedback loop, so too does the Daily Scrum. This is a daily Inspect and Adapt event that allows the team to quickly change course if something needs to be corrected and to make sure that they are on target to meet the Sprint Goal.

Sprint Review
The Sprint Review allows us to show work that was done within a Sprint to our stakeholders, in order to get their insight as to where we might be able to make our product better and to get them excited about what has been done and eager to put our product to use. Much of what we intend to do next in a Sprint comes from the Sprint Review! Without this, we are working blindly and hoping that we are truly adding the value our stakeholders desire.

The Sprint Review is <u>not</u> a demo, although it is often called one. The Developers should be demoing work to the Product Owner constantly throughout the Sprint, so they can get feedback quickly and make any necessary adjustments. The Product Owner should never be seeing work for the first time during the Sprint Review. The audience here is stakeholders, not each other, and we are only showing work that is already considered Done. The Sprint Review is where our stakeholders get to see our increment for the first time and provide valuable insight into what we have done and how well it meets their needs. The Product Owner drives the Sprint Review, although certainly members of the Developers may lead portions of the presentation.

Sprint Retrospective
The Sprint Retrospective is where the Scrum Team gets to talk about how the Sprint went and discuss how to make the next Sprint even better. This is one of the most important Inspect and Adapt events we have in our toolbox. The Sprint Retrospective can take many forms, but it should ultimately yield one or more action items that the team wants to take on during the next Sprint to improve how we work together. The Sprint Retrospective will get its own chapter later in this book.

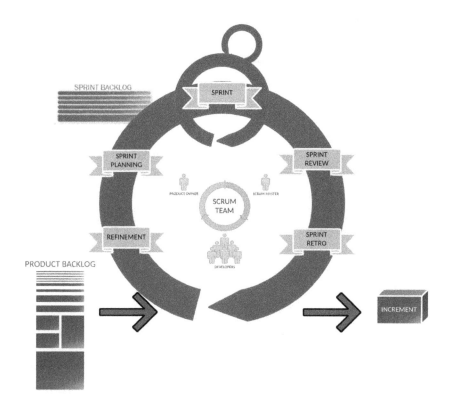

Figure 9 - The Scrum Roles, Events, and Artifacts

3 Artifacts

Product Backlog

The Product Backlog is the Product Owner's vision for the Product. It is maintained in real time and just-in-time to keep just enough work for the next several Sprints in scope. There should not be work in the backlog that the Product Owner doesn't feel will be touched for months. While it's important to keep track of that work for the future, it should be kept apart from the Product Backlog and only brought in as it gets close to a point where that work is valuable. The Product Backlog is a living artifact that is continually updated and ordered by the PO to make sure that the highest value items are always at the top. The Product Backlog acts as a medium-range view of the Product Roadmap, providing clarity into what is coming in the near future.

The Product Backlog regularly goes through Refinement to add detail and estimates, and to make sure that the Backlog is properly ordered. The act of Backlog Refinement is not considered a Scrum event, but it is crucial to the health of the Product Backlog.

Sprint Backlog
The Sprint Backlog is a child of the Product Backlog, consisting solely of PBIs that the Developers are forecasting to be Done in the current Sprint. The Developers can, and should, negotiate this with the Product Owner to make sure that the highest value items are getting worked on, while the Scrum Master serves as a check to ensure that the Developers don't commit to more work than they can fully accomplish. This is immediate-term planning that will result in an updated Product Increment.

Product Increment
The ultimate output of a Sprint is a Product Increment. This is a finite piece of Done work that has been fully reviewed by the Product Owner and stakeholders and _may_ be ready to be released into Production. Not every Product Increment is a Production Increment. The Product Increment delivers on the value promised by the Developers in accordance with the Sprint Goal and their Definition of Done.

Playing it Safe

A quick note on team safety is important before we continue, as it impacts the entire Scrum Team and our ability to succeed. Team safety is an important concept. The team should always feel like they it is safe to discuss important and difficult topics without fear. Team members should only be singled out if they are causing a disruption to the team, and never for failing to deliver work if they were met with genuine obstacles. The Scrum Team should be discussing how to remove those obstacles with the Scrum Master, not pointing fingers. Keeping the Scrum Values in mind at all times goes a long way toward building team safety. There should never be a lack of respect or trust among team members. Safety becomes extremely important when we are in an Inspect and Adapt cycle, and paramount during the Sprint Retrospective. The entire Scrum Team needs to be able to make critical decisions about what work they are doing and how they are doing it, without fear of reprisal.

A great Scrum Master always knows how to read the room and is attuned to whether or not the team feels safe. If he senses that team safety is low, he takes steps to remedy this by opening and guiding a discussion on how the entire Scrum Team can always work together to promote a sense of safety. Empiricism is impossible without a sense of safety. When the team does not feel safe, Transparency is quick to disappear, Inspect and Adapt activities are impaired, and the team starts to build silos around themselves. This behavior is not healthy for the team and should raise serious concerns. Team performance will suffer when this behavior is happening. Retrospectives will become quiet zones where nobody wants to talk because they do not feel safe in offering their opinions or observations.

There are obvious warning signs when team safety is low. Silence and lack of participation are the two most obvious ones. Giving safe and conservative answers when questions are asked is another. The chapter on Retrospectives will talk about team safety more, and go into ways you can actively work to improve (or create) it.

Is it Safe to Merge?

It's well established that there are exactly three roles in Scrum: Product Owner, Scrum Master, and Developers. Often, there is a natural desire to merge the role of Scrum Master with another role on the team. Should you do this, though?

The answer, as is so often the case, is it depends on your team. There is nothing in Scrum that demands the roles are taken up by different individuals.

Combining the Scrum Master role with a member of the Developers for many feels like the most natural approach. This keeps the Scrum Master not only embedded with the team, but already an integral part of what the team is doing from day to day. This can work under the right circumstances, but it short-changes the role of Scrum Master. If the SM/Dev is spending the majority of his day writing code or involved with testing, does he have a chance to truly take in everything that is happening with his team? How effective can he be at removing impediments? It's hard to function as a true servant-leader when you are a peer with the other members of the team.

What often happens when a member of the Developers takes on the Scrum Master role is that the team starts to do Scrum in name only. The events are performed, but there is typically little variation in how they take place. The Scrum Master often lacks the authority or will power to push the team beyond their perceived limits, and will be happy with the status quo. The ability to truly act as a change agent for the team and the organization can be restricted when wearing both hats at the same time. Both the Development and Scrum Master roles can be naturally diminished when one person wears both hats. For some teams, especially mature teams, this is all perfectly okay.

Combining the role of Scrum Master with that of the Product Owner, however, is perilous, as the two roles are designed to balance each other out in many ways. The Product Owner wants to deliver maximum value with every Sprint, the Scrum Master wants to make sure that the team doesn't over-commit when forecasting. The Product Owner often sees the Daily Scrum as a change to get the status of every Backlog Item in the Sprint, the Scrum Master knows this is a planning meeting for the Developers, and status updates are not necessary outside of that context. To put both hats on the same person creates a conflict and should be avoided.

Remember the responsibilities for each member of the Scrum Team: What, How, and Process. When you combine the Product Owner with the Scrum Master, you are giving her power over what the team works on and the process through which they accomplish it. That's a lot of power resting on one person's shoulders, and it will hamper the Developers' ability to decide how they are going to work.

None of this means you can't merge the roles. You can, and it might even work best for your teams. It's important, however, to think through exactly why you feel the need to merge the roles together, and what benefit you are immediately gaining by doing so. Scrum has an innate system of balance in place between the three roles; any time you double up a role with someone, you risk upsetting that balance. Consider the possible outcomes carefully and make the correct decision for your team.

Momentum

The... 'relay race' approach to product development...may conflict with the goals of maximum speed and flexibility. Instead a holistic or 'rugby' approach – where a team tries to go the distance as a unit, passing the ball back and forth – may better serve today's competitive requirements...

Moving the Scrum Downfield
From interviews with organization members from the CEO to young engineers, we learned that leading companies show six characteristics in managing their new product development processes:
1. Built-in instability
2. Self-organizing project teams
3. Overlapping development phases
4. "Multilearning"
5. Subtle control
6. Organizational transfer of learning

These characteristics are like pieces of a jigsaw puzzle. Each element, by itself, does not bring about speed and flexibility. But taken as a whole, the characteristics can produce a powerful new set of dynamics that will make a difference.[ix]

If you've ever wondered where 'Scrum' comes from, this is it. "The New New Product Development Game" published in 1986 first talked about "a holistic or 'rugby' approach -- where a team tries to go the distance as a unit, passing the ball back and forth..." and mentions the word "Scrum" as seen above. While this paper was talking about manufacturing, what it

51

proposed -- a radical new way of working -- transferred directly into what we now know as Scrum.

The ideas of built-in instability, self-organizing product teams, and "multilearning" are exactly the ways our Scrum Teams work. We accept that change is inevitable and we respond to it in rapid fashion. We want our teams to be self-organizing and self-managing; only they know how best to get work done. We want our teams to be T-shaped with a broad knowledge base and deep knowledge in specific areas. We encourage our team members to learn from each other, as well as from other teams and from leadership.

We empower our teams with absolute autonomy to make important decisions as to how to accomplish their work and the freedom to negotiate with the Product Owner when necessary to achieve their goals. We recognize that the three intrinsic goals of autonomy, mastery, and purpose drive great teams forward to make valuable product for our stakeholders. Our Scrum Teams are filled with exceptionally talented people, and they will prove it when given the freedom to determine how they work best as a team.

At the same time, we recognize that the organization as a whole must also change. The organization changes by way of overlapping development phases, subtle control, and an organizational transfer of learning. There is no hard stop in the development cycle where we halt everything and focus on hardening our code. This happens continuously, and we are always pushing ahead. Our teams can't stop delivering value, and we lead in a way that allows that to happen. The command-and-control structure becomes a thing of the past when we turn to an Agile mindset.

Waterfall – Each activity begins after the previous one is done

Scrum – Activities overlap and allow for rapid completion of work

Figure 10 - Scrum allows us to build and maintain momentum when compared to waterfall

Management becomes leadership and guides our teams along, supporting them in their work at every step. We recognize that the team's self-management skills are critical to their success and know how to take a step back and allow that to happen. We provide the teams with the knowledge they need to do their work and how to lead themselves with minimal intervention from leadership. We provide a space in which they are free to experiment and where it's safe to fail, because failure provides an opportunity for growth. As an organization, we take what we have learned from one or more teams and freely apply that knowledge to others where applicable. We aren't afraid to make mistakes either, as long as we learn from them. Leadership paves the road for success and lets the team find its way without interference.

By employing all six of these characteristics, we establish an Agile mentality in which Scrum can thrive. Like the 3-5-3 structure that Scrum is built upon, none of these are optional. These six things work together to form a base upon which we build. Building momentum to move the ball downfield -- Scrum -- happens because all of these things are valuable.

We build on this momentum by employing the cadence that Scrum demands. Every event in Sprint has a timebox, and the Scrum Master rigidly defends that limit. Every Sprint builds on the ones that came before it, and the entire Scrum Team is always working as a unit to move the Scrum downfield. Without any of the pieces -- whether the six characteristics just presented here or the elements of the 3-5-3 structure -- we will stall and have to work to regain momentum.

Done

The word "Done" might be one of the single most important words we use in Scrum. It's important to know what we are doing, but it's equally -- if not more important -- to know when we get there. This is where having a Definition of Done (DoD) comes into play. Every team should have a Definition of Done that clearly indicates what the entire Scrum Team acknowledges must be conformed to before any work in a Sprint Backlog can be called Done. The DoD gets the entire Scrum Team aligned as to what constitutes a completed Backlog Item and makes sure that everyone is speaking the same language. It brings clarity to the increment and assures that the product will be in a potentially releasable state when the Sprint ends. If you are hearing the phrase "It's Done, but..." then you need to work on what exactly the word 'Done' means to your team.

PRODUCT OWNER

SCRUM MASTER

DONE!

DEVELOPERS

Figure 11 - The Scrum Team works together to define Done

The factors that go into your team's DoD will vary, depending on the organization and the individual Scrum Team's maturity and technical expertise. Things that will often factor into a DoD are:

- Code complete and unit tested.
- All acceptance criteria have been met.
- Code coverage meets the agreed upon threshold.
- Code has been integration tested by developers.
- Code has been checked in with clear comments.
- Code does not break the build.
- Code has been peer-reviewed and accepted.
- Item has been tested by QE with no major defects.
- Item has been reviewed by the Product Owner and the increment has been accepted.

- All appropriate end-user documentation has been written and reviewed.
- Code has been released into production.

Getting to Done is a journey that the team undertakes together. During Sprint Planning, the DoD assists the team in forecasting work that can be done without sacrificing quality. The DoD, like much of what we do in Scrum, is always subject to the Inspect and Adapt cycle, and will mature over time. A team without a DoD doesn't have to do everything at once, but just start with a few basic items and add to it over time. You should have a copy of the DoD displayed somewhere for the team to always see. I have a poster at my desk with the DoD for my team that can't be missed by anyone walking past. Done happens in real time. Backlog Items are constantly moving from one state to the next as they go from not started into development into testing and into production.

It can be challenging to enforce the DoD with a team that is newly formed. Team PAWS is struggling with defining what Done means to them and how to adhere to it. Recognizing what is happening, James has stepped in to help facilitate matters. He knows that the first step is to empower the entire team. He makes sure they are working together to pick only a couple of the most important criteria to start. James coaches the team to consider the increment from the perspective of the entire team and not just think about their own work. He knows that just telling the team they are empowered doesn't make it so, and he works to make them all feel like they own their DoD. The team agreed that while they would like to have two peers review all code, pair programming is sufficient for now. They decide to defer having an additional reviewer until later in their product's lifecycle when they feel more comfortable with that.

The DoD and acceptance criteria are not the same. Acceptance criteria help to clearly define what the PO is looking for and drive testing efforts to make sure they are satisfied. They will often mirror test cases using a "Given...When...Then" structure to provide clarity, but this is not always so. Given the example DoD above, the increment isn't considered Done until it has been released into Production. For Team PAWS who is working on a green-field project that will take several Sprints to have a viable MVP, nothing will be released to production for some time, so they do not make that part of their DoD. They still have acceptance criteria in each Product Backlog Item that help everyone to understand what will make each Item considered Done. The distinction between the two is an important one. They also recognize that they will not likely have any end-user documentation until later in their development cycle, and agree to defer that from their DoD until later. They are hoping to bring in an additional team member with strong technical writing skills to assist with that aspect of their product.

WIP limits can also help out greatly. We are very good at knowing when something isn't started, and with a well-maintained DoD, we are pretty good at knowing when something is complete. As a rule, we are pretty lousy at knowing a whole lot in between those two states. We know we are working on it but not necessarily how far we are to completion. WIP limits help us to not take on too much work simultaneously. It's easier and better to get five things Done than to get ten things partway complete. It is incredibly easy for incomplete work to pile up. Scrum will help expose where these bottlenecks are, force the team to talk about them, and come up with ideas on how to solve them. One of the most common bottlenecks is getting code from the developers to the testers in a timely fashion. Excellent continuous integration and continuous deployment practices will help solve this, but sometimes it's just not that easy. When work piles up like this, it becomes increasingly simple for the team to unwittingly take on Technical Debt, and soon they find themselves busy trying to dig out rather than focusing on adding new value to the product. Enforcing your DoD along with excellent engineering practices will help prevent this from becoming a roadblock for your teams.

How Long Can This Keep Going On?

The Scrum Guide says that a Sprint is timeboxed to one month or less. It's already been noted that Sprint length may vary from one team to another, even within the same organization. Sprints should be long enough for the team to deliver value but short enough to minimize risk of delaying the release of an increment. The entire Scrum Team should agree on how long their Sprint should be, unless there is a standard throughout the organization that is agreed upon.

I have personally been on Scrum Teams with one-week, two-week, and four-week Sprints. All have different things that make them excellent choices, depending on what variables are at work. The most common Sprint length is two weeks long, by a factor of almost triple the next closest Sprint length. There are good reasons to stick to two weeks. When looking at the larger factors of quality, responsiveness, productivity, and predictability, a two-week Sprint provides the most balanced approach. Performance is at or near the top of all categories with two-week iterations.

Longer sprints will yield higher quality and predictability, while shorter Sprints will provide greater responsiveness and productivity. These are not universal truths, of course, but the trends are certainly there. This makes sense. When working in a one-week Sprint, we expect the team to be highly responsive and productive given the shorter timebox. This speed is hard to sustain, and the potential for defects grows as the team is working quickly. Longer Sprints mean that the team is less responsive in general, and seems less productive given the longer timebox. These teams have more time to focus on the quality of their code and can work at a highly predictable velocity. Finding the sweet spot at two or three weeks tends to strike the best balance between the two extremes. I recommend starting with a two-week Sprint and sticking with that for several iterations before changing Sprint length. Every change means disruption to the team, and you want to minimize that impact.

The other pattern that teams will fall victim to early is the idea of extending a Sprint so that they can get everything finished. Don't do it. The Sprint provides a steady cadence to our work and we rely on that rhythm for everything else to fall neatly into place. It's better to move unfinished work into the Product Backlog (from where it may well be put directly into the new Sprint) and discuss in the Retrospective why the Scrum Team could not get everything done. Were they overzealous with how much they thought they could do? Were there unforeseen interruptions; problems with builds or deployments, or help desk issues that consumed time that was not planned for? Having the open discussion in a Retrospective and making improvements, while keeping the Sprint timebox intact, is far healthier for your team than artificially extending a Sprint just to get everything done. The entire point of the timebox is that everything starts and stops exactly as planned with no option. Keep in mind that the next Sprint begins the very second the current Sprint ends. There is literally no gap between them. If it's the first day of a new Sprint and the team wants to extend the previous one, it is already too late. That Sprint is over.

It's important to also gauge how frequently you can release an increment into the market. It's not required that there be a release at the end of every Sprint, but the increment that is Done should be potentially releasable should the Product Owner wish it.

On Team PAWS, Sarah knows that because this is a new product, she will go several iterations before she has a viable release candidate, and she is okay with this. Her roadmap allows several Sprints before she has what she feels is a Minimum Viable Product (MVP). Once released, she hopes to put out new functionality at least every four weeks, constantly adding value to the app and getting feedback from users on what they still need, or what else they want to see the app do. The fixed length of Sprints and the velocity of her team allow her insight into when she can get a release to market and have faith in the quality of that release. Sarah has her roadmap built out and has a general idea of what Minimum Marketable Features (MMFs) she needs in the product beyond the initial launch. She also knows that around the end of the year her team will all be taking extra time off around the holidays. To keep on cadence during that time, she and the team agreed that they would double their two-week Sprint to four weeks to allow for time off, while still keeping to their basic cadence.

Pick your Sprint length wisely and stick to it. Altering the length of a Sprint even by a day will throw your cadence off. Exceptions made around the holidays are normal, but they are just that; exceptions.

Feeling Defective

Defects are a fact of life, or at least a fact of software development. As much as we all try to write perfect code every time, some defects are bound to slip through the cracks. As we work on complex systems there are bound to be some things that go wrong. This doesn't mean that the Developers are bad, it just means that our systems are complicated and we are human. We try to automate our unit tests and account for everything before it leaves development, but sometimes we just miss.

When we plan our Sprints, we might have a few defects in the Product Backlog that need to be addressed, but more are bound to come to light as our exceptional QE Teams put our software through its paces. Scrum demands engineering excellence from our Developers, and how we handle defects is absolutely part of being Agile.

There are essentially two types of defects:
- Defects that are directly related to Sprint Backlog Items
- Defects that are part of other systems we are not currently working on

We handle these two types of defects in different ways because their nature demands it. If we find defects that are directly related to a Sprint Backlog Item, the way forward is a simple one. In keeping with our commitment to producing clean code in accordance with our Definition of Done, we fix these defects immediately. These defects are essentially just new tasks for our Backlog Items. We add a new sticky note in the swim lane for that Backlog Item for the task (or enter a virtual one on our digital tool), and the team works on rapidly getting the defect fixed and back to QE for testing. We cannot mark these Backlog Items as Done until we have completed them and QE has signed off. This should be a part of a good Definition of Done. Under no circumstances should the Developers sacrifice their standards of quality and excellence.

What should not happen when a defect is found on a Sprint Backlog Item is re-estimating the item to account for the additional work. The estimate stands as a complete picture of getting that item to Done and should include coding, testing, and any potential rework required to fix issues that arise. Nor do we separate the defect from the Backlog Item that spawned it. Fixing this defect is a part of completing the work and should never be tracked separately where it can potentially be lost in the larger Product Backlog and forgotten about. Remember that the earlier in the cycle we find a defect, the less it costs for us to fix it; a defect found in production is exponentially more expensive than one found in development!

There may be individual cases in which your organization's risk aversion or willingness will supersede this. A defect might be found that is an extreme edge case or is considered so minor that the product can go live with it and it will be fixed in the future. This is part of the negotiation with the Product Owner, who ultimately can make that decision. If it is determined that the risk of not releasing outweighs the risk of shipping with the bug intact, go ahead and enter that defect into the Product Backlog.

Defects that are outside of a Sprint Backlog Item should be entered in the Product Backlog and prioritized based on their value by the Product Owner. These should be estimated and taken into future Sprints as planned work, just as we would accept any other Product Backlog Item. These Backlog Items will make their way to the top of the Product Backlog as they become important and valuable, and can be discussed during Sprint Planning and addressed along with new work coming in.

If you use separate defect tracking software, putting defects into the Product Backlog might feel redundant, and you wouldn't necessarily be wrong. I would argue that all the defect needs on the Product Backlog is a placeholder that points to the actual defect in your tracking software, and there's no need to clutter up the board with redundant information. It's important that everything the team touches be visible in their Sprint Backlog, however. Not even listing a placeholder Item for a defect means you no longer have a single version of truth that reflects the team's entire activity. Keep the details in your defect tracking software if you have one; put them in the Backlog Item if you don't. Don't let one stand in the way of the other. There should never be two separate backlogs.

It's worth pointing out that a defect is not a User Story. User Stories are a great way of writing Product Backlog Items, but they are by no means mandatory. For defects, they actually are fairly useless. "As a user I want this bug fixed so my software works" is not a great User Story. A good defect report should have certain things that make them of maximum use to everyone:

- A clear title describing the defect
- Simple steps to reliably reproduce the bug repeatedly
- Expected and observed results
- The version the defect was found in
- Screenshots if applicable
- Only one defect per report

One way of making sure there is enough room to deal with uncertainty related to potential defects is to build a buffer into your Sprint to allow for unplanned work. If the team can deliver 30 points, leave 5 points aside for unplanned activities. This might not be defect-related but could be support activities or other work that was simply unforeseen during Sprint Planning. This buffer leaves the team a way to handle the unexpected without risking blowing up the Sprint because there is now too much work to get everything done.

Having the buffer in place also helps you to insulate the team against 100% utilization. Trying to max out the team to their full effort during planning is setting up the team for a potential disaster. There is always some work that wasn't initially planned for, and we don't want to put the Sprint Goal at risk simply because we could not think of everything up front. That is predictive, waterfall behavior. Leaving a buffer allows your Developers room for the unexpected.

V - What's the Plan?

"[Gantt Charts] have become works of art. Every single step in a project is laid out in detail… These charts are truly impressive to behold. The only problem with them is that they are always, always wrong." -- Jeff Sutherland[x]

Agile Means We Don't Plan, Right?

I have lost track of the number of times I have heard this from teams new to Scrum. It seems that somewhere along the way this myth has taken hold and has become somewhat pervasive among people who haven't been exposed to how Scrum is truly supposed to work. Several times I have been asked to work with a new team and this is the first thing I hear. Developers get excited because they start to think they can just start coding without waiting for any requirements to take shape. New Product Owners are nervous because they don't know how to communicate the plan to the team, because they don't have the safety of the Business Requirements Document.

The world of waterfall meant we plan everything before doing anything. The BRD meant we knew everything up-front before we wrote a single line of code, and it was frozen in time, never to be changed. Our Business Analysts and Project Managers needed to be psychic and try to predict where the market would be in the future and what things our customers might want, without necessarily talking to them. The BRD created a false sense of safety that we knew everything before we started working and all expectations were clearly established. We've accepted that this was not a best practice (in most cases). We know that the BRD became obsolete quickly as the market changed. Often it took us months, if not years, to deliver everything in the requirements, and by then customers' needs were no longer what they once were. Because Agile is perceived as "anti-waterfall," I believe the idea took hold that Agile must mean that we just start working without a plan and everything will fall into place. This is a drastic misreading of the Agile Manifesto at best, and a disaster waiting to happen at worst.

Here's the truth of it: We actually plan all the time in Scrum, it's just that we don't always call it that. So how does it all work exactly? Sprint Planning is the only event that explicitly has the word "Plan" in it. Obviously, this is time spent that we dedicate to the fine art of planning something. In fact, all the other events in Scrum involve planning at some level as well, within the context of the Sprint itself. The Daily Scrum meeting is a 24-hour Inspect and Adapt event; one that demands we discuss the previous day and make a new plan for the day ahead based on what we now know. The Sprint Review is a planning event during which we get information directly from our stakeholders and prepare to incorporate that feedback into our future Sprints. The Sprint Retrospective is where we plan how we are going to work as a team to get even better as we move forward. These events all demand the three pillars of Empiricism are in place, and we are ready to Adapt at each one.

Scrum gives us a bunch of small feedback loops where we can gain new insight and re-plan. If we never plan, we will fall into the same traps that waterfall gave us -- never moving forward but just treading water amidst a sea of change. It is this ability to adapt -- to look honestly at how we are doing and make adjustments -- that makes Scrum work. Planning constantly gives us an edge over teams that are not able to do so, and allows us to deliver value to our customers quickly. Change can be scary. In Scrum we embrace the change and recognize that the best way to deliver high-quality product to our customers quickly is through these small, rapid feedback loops. We get information from the stakeholders; we turn it around quickly and we show it to them. We get their feedback and we make the necessary adaptations to our plan to accommodate their new requests and requirements. We repeat this cycle until we have exactly what our customers desire, and we release it to them rapidly.

We recognize that planning is important, but we know that our plans are subject to change the moment we put them into action, and we accept that volatility. Through our ability to re-plan every workday, we make sure we are using our time to its utmost, focusing on precisely the most important things we need to do to drive value. Change is no longer something to be afraid of but something to be embraced.

Responding to Change Over Following a Plan

This is the phrase from the Agile Manifesto that causes confusion: "That is, while there is value in the items on the right, we value the items on the left more." It doesn't say we don't care about what's on the right; just that it is less valuable than what is on the left.

It is this part that gets lost in translation somewhere.

We still very much need to have a plan, but it's a plan that is written in wet sand and the tide is coming in. Our plan is very much subject to change -- and often -- as we get into the work and begin to fully realize the tasks we have committed to during a Sprint. Anything that is planned out beyond the current Sprint is nebulous at best and WILL change when we get to Sprint Planning. Scrum puts emphasis on the act of planning often over rigidly following a plan that is set in stone. The fact is that our plan can change several times a day, and we need to constantly be able to re-plan based on the new knowledge we have acquired. We know that our plan will become obsolete almost the moment we finish it. The art of Sprint Planning lies in minimizing the time spent doing the following:
- Analyzing things that may never happen.
- Analyzing to an impossible degree of accuracy.

When I talk about Sprint Planning with my teams for the first time, I will often show them the most famous World of Warcraft video ever made -- Leeroy Jenkins. For those who somehow have never seen it, it shows the group of players coming up with an elaborate plan for how they will tackle something in the game, right down to a 33.3 (repeating, of course) percent chance of success. All of this is discussed while Leeroy himself is AFK. No sooner do they finish the plan when Leeroy returns, shouts out a battle cry and runs into the room, blowing the whole thing up. Everyone dies in a sea of profanity as the plan goes completely out the window. It's hysterical. It's important to plan, but getting to that level of detail is only time wasted because once someone starts the work -- and they Leeroy your plan -- all bets are off and you need to be able to respond to those changes quickly. Scrum values the act of planning far more than the actual plans, because we recognize those are highly volatile.

One other mistake I have seen is that people want to rush through Sprint Planning. This is an important core event in Scrum, and it's critical that we don't undervalue it. Remember that Sprint Planning can take up to eight hours for a 4-week Sprint! That's one full work day dedicated to planning out what we are going to do. For a 2-week Sprint -- not an uncommon Sprint length -- it's still up to four hours of planning. That is not a small amount of time, and trying to rush through it in an hour so we can "do real work" is doing the Scrum Team a disservice.

Sprint Planning is when we review everything that we have learned in the Sprint Review and Sprint Retrospective, take a hard look at what is in our Product Backlog, and come up with our best forecast of all the work the Developers will be able to accomplish during this Sprint.

PRODUCT BACKLOG

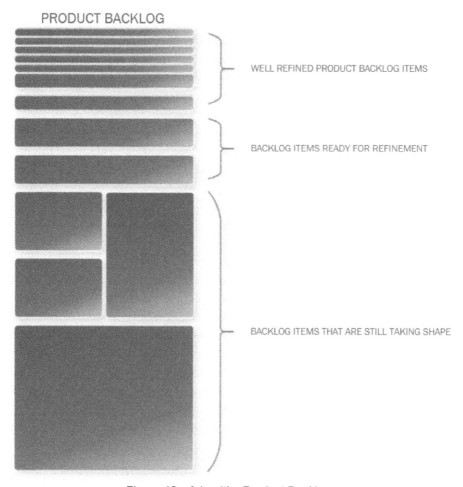

WELL REFINED PRODUCT BACKLOG ITEMS

BACKLOG ITEMS READY FOR REFINEMENT

BACKLOG ITEMS THAT ARE STILL TAKING SHAPE

Figure 12 - A healthy Product Backlog

We have two questions to answer during Sprint Planning:
- What can be done during this Sprint?
- How will the work we have chosen get done?

To answer the first question, we have to carefully examine all of the information we have coming in:
- The Product Backlog content
- The Developers' historic velocity
- The Developers' capacity for this Sprint
- What work can be pulled in to create a valuable increment of software

The second part of Sprint Planning is where the Developers start to seriously deconstruct the work, come up with design and architecture decisions, and break down work into more manageable tasks.

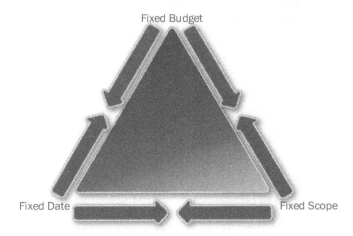

Fixed Budget

Fixed Date

Fixed Scope

Figure 13 - Avoid getting locked into the Iron Triangle of Fixed Budget, Date, and Scope

Sprint Planning is the perfect time to negotiate with the Product Owner and make sure that what the team is forecasting will be delivering a valuable increment. Nobody wants to work on something that is going to be thrown away, or is just there to keep us busy while we wait for important work to come. In most cases, budget will be pre-determined for a product (or iteration) and the Scrum Team will not have much flexibility on adjusting it. That leaves Date and Scope as items that are completely within the Scrum Team's ability to influence. This is where good estimation and solid knowledge of the product become crucial to your Sprint Planning. By focusing on where the value is, and having an honest, transparent discussion with the Product Owner, we can plan to do great things in every Sprint.

Shaping the Backlog

Because the Product Backlog is a living artifact that reflects the Product Owner's near-term vision for the product as a whole, it's important that we fully understand the lifecycle of a Product Backlog Item and how the Product Owner can assign value.

Typically, anyone can enter a new Product Backlog Item, although this may vary. Nothing goes into a ready state, however, without the Product Owner's seal of approval. She is the absolute authority over what lives in the Product Backlog and the order of all items there. The Product Backlog is then ordered by the business value of each item, with the high-value, fully refined items at the very top. Nobody can remove a Product Backlog Item except for the Product Owner, unless specifically asked by the PO to do so.

A Product Backlog items usually follows an informal flow before it makes it to the backlog, as illustrated below:

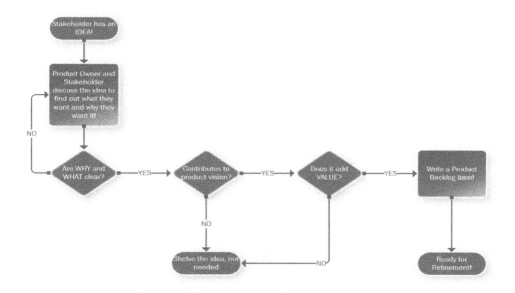

Figure 14 - Getting from Idea to Product Backlog Item

Someone comes to the Product Owner with an idea. This could be a stakeholder, a member of the Developers, or even the Product Owner herself thinking of something exciting. For the sake of this example, we will assume a stakeholder going forward. The Product Owner has a conversation with the stakeholder to fully understand the idea. At this point, the Product Owner has to ask certain questions as to WHAT the

69

idea is and WHY it is needed. The conversation with the stakeholder must continue until these questions have been fully answered to the Product Owner's satisfaction.

Once the initial conversations are done, the Product Owner has new things to consider:
- Does this idea contribute to her product vision?
- Does this idea add value to the product?

If one or both of these answers is no, the idea should be shelved where it can be revisited in the future. Do not just discard the idea, however. Just because it doesn't add to the vision or value now doesn't mean it won't in a few months. The Product Owner should revisit these shelved ideas on a regular basis to see if and how they align with the larger product. Once it becomes clear that the idea does add to the product, a Product Backlog Item is created for this idea. One item is sufficient; it will be refined by the Scrum Team and will be split into smaller stories as the time comes. The idea will typically move into a slot near the bottom of the Product Backlog and will move up over time as additional refinement happens.

Assigning value is important and challenging. As new work emerges during a Sprint, items will invariably be added to the Product Backlog (or even the Sprint Backlog) that take priority over what was already there. Value decisions need to be made, often in real time, and items will constantly shift in value throughout their time on the Product Backlog, and the order of items will change accordingly. How the Product Owner assigns value is entirely up to her. She makes a decision of what is most important and valuable for the product, and acts based on that decision. Nobody can change the order of Product Backlog Items except for the PO. Value can be assigned using a point system, by putting numbers or stickers on a physical card, or just by changing their position on the list using a digital tool.

The Product Owner's word as to what is in the Product Backlog and the order of those items is absolute and final. These decisions must be respected by the entire organization. That doesn't mean that if the CEO comes to the PO and says, "I need this," that the Product Owner should just say "No." She is empowered to say, "This Sprint is fully loaded, but the Developers and I will see where we have the capacity for this, and I will let you know in which Sprint we can make it happen!"

Looking at the Product Backlog diagram, we see small, well-refined stories toward the top. These stories are ready for the Developers to discuss in Sprint Planning and add to their Sprint Backlog. Following those initial small stories, we have larger ones with a clear idea of what is needed, and these stories are now ready for refinement. After that are the newer stories that are still relatively vague. These are ones where the Product Owner has an idea of what is needed but needs to spend time refining it herself, possibly breaking it into smaller stories before the team even sees them, and making sure they are in a condition where refinement can happen. The farther down the backlog we move, the less clear and larger our items become. You should see this pattern take place within your Product Backlog; it's a clear sign that the backlog is healthy.

Sarah aggressively refines her Product Backlog. The conversations she has with customers and stakeholders provide her with valuable insight into their needs and what the market is looking for from Team PAWS. She takes all of that information and adds to her Product Backlog features and Backlog Items that the Developers will refine further and eventually turn into working software. She manages her release schedule based on everything she knows about her product and at which points there will be sufficient value added to get a release out the door. She spends up to eight hours of her two-week Sprint just focusing on her Product Backlog, alone or with the team.

Bringing the Daily Scrum to Life

At its heart, the Daily Scrum is the simplest of meetings, but it's also one of the easiest to get wrong. There are many anti-patterns that I have seen firsthand with the Daily Scrum, all of which are easy to solve with a little discipline. It's important that we first know what the Daily Scrum should be before we start to look at potential trouble spots.

Simply put, the Daily Scrum is an internal meeting for the Developers to discuss where they are currently and what the plan is over the next 24 hours to progress toward the Sprint Goal. The Daily Scrum is timeboxed to fifteen minutes and is held at the same time and place each day. That's it. How the Daily Scrum is run can vary, but it all comes down to those two sentences. Some teams like to use the Three Question format and go around the room; some prefer to talk about work on a PBI-by-PBI basis; and others just have an open discussion of the plan every day without any strict format. These are all perfectly valid approaches to the Daily Scrum. The important thing is that the team meets daily to Inspect and Adapt, and come up with a new plan for the coming day. I have had equal success with all three of these variations, depending on the individual team.

It's important to note that the "three questions" format is no longer considered an important practice during the Daily Scrum. What is important is that the team is planning their next 24 hours of work, and that conversation can take any form that is comfortable for the team. Nobody has to "go next."

It's important to note that this is a Developers only meeting. The Scrum Master and Product Owner are not required for the Daily Scrum and have no voice in the meeting unless the Developers have a question. The same applies to stakeholders who wish to be present -- they are welcome to listen if the team allows it, but they cannot disrupt the meeting. It is incumbent upon the Scrum Master to make sure the Developers are not disrupted by anyone. Not even the CEO can interrupt a Daily Scrum! Many teams have a "16th minute" for questions and discussion after the formal Daily Scrum has ended, and that works for those teams. As a Scrum Master, your job is to make sure that the Daily Scrum happens and to be present to help facilitate if needed. Early in a Scrum Team's transformation, your presence and guidance are likely to be required. A mature team will have their Daily Scrum without your presence, and without you having to actively gather everyone. It simply becomes second nature.

It's also important that this is not a status report. The team should be having an open conversation amongst themselves; they are not checking in with the Scrum Master, the Product Owner, or stakeholders. If you find that the Developers are addressing you directly all the time, turn and face away from the team so they are talking to your back, while still actively listening to the conversation. You aren't there to get an update from everyone. This type of Daily Scrum quickly becomes increasingly useless, and team members are less engaged than if they are simply having an internal discussion. We never want the Daily Scrum to become about feeding information to someone outside of the Developers. As Scrum Masters or Product Owners, it's easy to interject ourselves into the discussion and start to ask leading questions. Save those for the 16th minute.

All of the Developers have a chance to speak. If you are facilitating a Daily Scrum and notice that one person is often merely standing there silently, ask him/her to start the discussion. If you find that the meeting is becoming stale and members are seeing the Daily Scrum as a waste of time, that's a signal that you might need to try something different. If the team is used to simply going around the room and answering the three questions, try walking the board and talking about each PBI one at a time until everyone has spoken. If that isn't working, to start things off ask an open-ended question about what the plan is for the day and then simply stand back and let the team talk. This is their opportunity to make rapid adaptations. Let them make full use of their 15 minutes! There may be team members who feel like they get nothing from the Daily Scrum; that's your cue to mix things up and get them involved. Members should be listening to the discussion, not tuning out because they feel it is 15 minutes wasted. This is their meeting and they should feel completely empowered. Keeping outsiders from the meeting, or making sure they are not disruptive, is a good way to help empower the team. When they feel like it's just reporting to someone, the energy and purpose of the meeting can quickly become lost.

Don't allow the meeting to become repetitive. I have had teams go into their Daily Scrum and every single day without fail, they spoke in the exact same order, often giving the exact same "update" as the day before. One day, I walked in with one color of Planning Poker cards and made everyone draw a card as they entered the room. We went from lowest to highest, purely at random based on who drew what card. This alone was enough to change the dynamic in the room as they now had to figure out who went next, and the discussion that started took a different shape.

Keep your team's working agreement visible during the Daily Scrum if you find there are problems. It helps greatly to have the meeting in front of the board, so individual Backlog Items can be referenced and discussed in detail if needed. If you don't use a physical board, then a projector or monitor displaying the digital board you are using is more than sufficient, and it gives the team easy talking points as they plan their day.

Talk about the Sprint Goal during the Daily Scrum. Be sure to ask the team how they feel they are progressing and the likelihood of achieving their goal. You don't have to ask this every day, but it's definitely good to take the temperature of the room a few times during a Sprint. If the Goal is at risk, this should be turned into an opportunity to Inspect, Adapt, and negotiate with the Product Owner, if necessary, to get back on track.

It's important that everyone walks out of the Daily Scrum with a clear idea of what the plan is. If there is any doubt, ask that exact question near the end of the meeting -- particularly if you sense that the team is checking out. There should be clear expectations of what is going to be done that day, and where the team should be in 24 hours. It's okay to miss that target – things happen – but as with everything else in Scrum, it's important that we have a plan.

It's become a common practice that everyone on the team must stand during the Daily Scrum. Go back and check the Scrum Guide. There's nothing in there about standing, and the meeting is not formally called the "Daily Stand-up", although that is a common name used by Scrum Teams. For many teams, the Daily Scrum happens online with everyone's camera turned on; I guarantee they are not all standing. If your team doesn't all stand during the Daily Scrum, but is doing everything else exactly right, don't die on that hill. It literally makes no difference in how the team performs.

One more note on the Daily Scrum. Keep that 15-minute timebox in mind and stick to it. This will take some effort with new teams as they adjust to working this way. If you sense that the team's discussion is going off track and they are not going to finish in time, feel free to put that topic in a parking lot and come back to it in the "16th minute." Let the majority of the team go when the timebox has expired and only those who need to continue the discussion should remain behind if necessary. Don't allow 16th minute discussions to become the norm, however, or you have defeated the entire point of the 15-minute timebox.

How Much Planning is Enough?

I Love it When a Plan Comes Together

Sprint Planning is a big deal, and it requires a significant amount of time from the Scrum Team. But how much planning do we have to get accomplished, and to what level of detail? It's important that we come out of Sprint Planning with a clear picture of what we expect the Sprint to look like and how we will execute the plan. But we cannot plan for absolutely everything, nor should we even try to. The exact right amount of planning may vary from Sprint to Sprint, but ultimately it comes down to just enough to get us started, and let the rest of it emerge during the Sprint.

The three elements of a user story, or any Product Backlog Item, are Card, Conversation, and Confirmation[xi]. This is a practice that emerged from Extreme Programming (XP) and has carried forward as a best practice regardless of the framework we are using. We need all three of these elements to have a good user story, but we don't need them all up front!

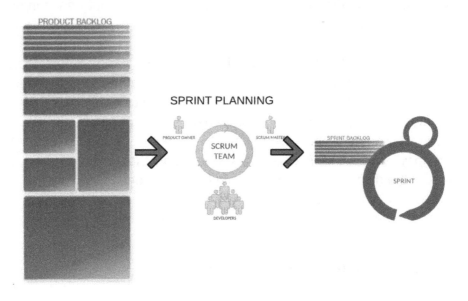

Figure 15 - Sprint Planning and the two Backlogs

The Card is the beginning of all user stories. Every item in our Product Backlog has a card. We write them on a physical card or sticky note, or we enter them using a digital card in the tool used by our organization. The card is essentially a pointer to the entire story, containing just enough information to get us started and remind the Developers of what we are trying to accomplish.   Notes are written on it as the description is fleshed out, and we have our effort estimate and priority reflected somewhere on the card. The card is where our story lives, and it drives everything else forward.

Skipping ahead, Confirmation tells us how we know we have satisfied all of the conditions for this user story. These are the acceptance criteria and tests for the user story, and give us a significant milestone on our Definition of Done. Without a clearly defined confirmation as communicated from the customer via the Product Owner, we cannot measure if we have delivered the expected value for this user story. The confirmation is clearly written out, typically on the back of the card, or in the appropriate field in your digital tool. Things like use cases, mockups or full design documents are sometimes useful, but not truly a part of your confirmation data (although they might be part of your Definition of Done, depending on your team and organization).

The Conversation is where the bulk of our planning happens. The card has just enough information for us to have a conversation. Keeping the Agile Manifesto in mind, we value "individuals and interactions over processes and tools," and "the most efficient and effective method of conveying information to and within a development team is face-to-face conversation." The card gets us started but the conversation moves us forward. We may – and will – add information to the card with more details as they emerge, but the only way they emerge is by having those conversations. The Developers must be talking to each other constantly as they work together to deliver value. The Product Owner and the Developers must be in regular conversation to negotiate scope, to further refine the Developers' understanding of any Backlog Item, and to make sure that the correct value is being created for the customer. Developers should be unafraid to show in-progress work to the Product Owner to get feedback early and often. The business and the customer are in regular discussion with the Product Owner to discuss their wants and needs, and help the Product Owner identify where there is value to be added to our products. Conversation is key to everything. The sweet spot is where everyone gets just enough information, just in time, to deliver the value required.

Clearly we can't have all of these conversations during Sprint Planning, and that's okay. It's important that when we plan, we allow room for flexibility. It is impossible for the team to think of absolutely everything during the timebox we have set aside for Sprint Planning. There are always unexpected tasks or work that we think is needed that turns out not to be. We can't plan on a certain number of defects per Backlog Item, because we haven't written the code yet. Of course, we always strive for zero! Talking about the most important tasks in fairly broad terms is usually just enough detail to start additional conversation, and that's exactly enough. If you identify the major pieces of work during Sprint Planning, but leave the smaller pieces for future conversation, the Developers have probably identified the majority of the work they need to do to complete that Backlog Item. The time spent getting into minute detail is probably time wasted at that point.

The Utilization Myth

"Every line of code costs money to write and more money to support. It is better for the developers to be surfing than writing code that won't be needed. If they write code that is ultimately not used, I will be paying for that code for the life of the system, which is typically longer than my professional life. If they went surfing, they would have fun, and I would have a less expensive system to maintain." -- Jeff Sutherland[xii]

It is also very important that we avoid the mistake of 100% utilization in our Sprints. Leaving the team room, as discussed in the section about defects, gives them the space they need to experiment, to fix defects, and to handle the unexpected. The rule I have lived by is that we plan for 80% of 80%; 64% utilization, if you don't want to do the math. Nobody is going to be completely on focus 100% of the time. There are unexpected interruptions in our work day -- be it someone stopping by our desk, attending to email, or simply getting up to use the restroom. The first 80% accounts for this time. By factoring in the second 80%, we allow room for experimentation, for unplanned work, and for the added flexibility that our Developers require. Chances are, your teams will be able to deliver more than 64% of their velocity per Sprint, but giving them that flexibility allows them room to deliver maximum value. Remember the mantra of "under-commit, over-deliver." Of course, you also need to make adjustments in the base velocity number to account for vacations and holidays, and then derive your target number from there.

Load your Sprints up to around that magical number of 64% and leave the team room. They will use it without being overburdened. Don't try to plan down to every minute detail, but allow ample room for conversation. If you're sitting with your team and nobody is talking, that isn't always a good sign! You might even find that you don't need the entire timebox for Sprint Planning, and everyone can get back to work more quickly than expected!

Expecting the Developers to be on task 100% of the time leads to undesirable results. Burnout is the most obvious. If we are going all out, all the time, performance is going to suffer and morale will rapidly decline. We need to let our team members have space to breathe, and not suffocate them under unrealistic expectations. Forcing them to always be busy leads to sloppy work, or work that is not needed as they find things to simply stay busy. You're better off letting them go surfing.

We are Quite Refined

Before Sprint Planning even happens, Backlog Refinement is necessary. Backlog Refinement is NOT one of the official five Scrum Events, but it's vital to the health of the Product Backlog. At its heart, the Product Backlog is a living artifact. Backlog Items move in and out at all times, and the Product Backlog provides a real-time snapshot of the work that needs to be done in upcoming Sprints. Before Sprint Planning can occur, Backlog Refinement should take place to get the stories in as close to a Ready state as possible. We don't need to get them exactly perfect during the refinement process, however.

Per the Scrum Guide, Backlog Refinement can take up to 10% of the Sprint. That's a full eight hours in a two-week Sprint! That doesn't necessarily mean it is all time spent with the entire Scrum Team in a room hashing everything out. Some of this time is dedicated just to the Product Owner refining Product Backlog Items as she understands them, before bringing them to the Developers for additional refinement. The Product Owner should own the refinement process, working with the Developers as much as is needed. The Scrum Master is there to facilitate and assist with the process, but refinement can take place without the Scrum Master's presence. Refinement is ideally not a just-in-time activity. You should be aiming to refine work that is a couple of Sprints out, so that the top of the Product Backlog is always in a ready state.

The refinement process comes down to three basic things:
- Asking questions to better our understanding of Product Backlog Items.

- Splitting large Backlog Items into smaller, more easily deliverable chunks.
- Estimating the effort to get each PBI to Done.

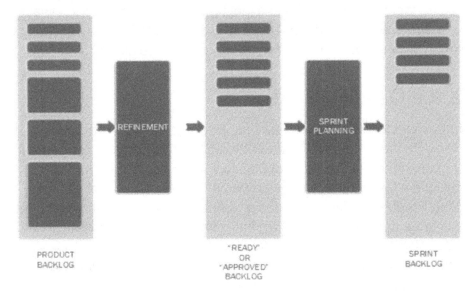

Figure 16 - Refining the Product Backlog

Asking questions is the Conversation part of any Backlog Item. The Product Owner should explain her vision and what she is looking for in this Backlog Item. The Developers should then ask questions and discuss what is there in as much detail as is needed to flesh out the story further and understand what is needed. The conversation is critical to the entire process, as we have already seen. The Developers should always be asking one important question:

"How do we make this smaller while still retaining value?"

This is where the activity of splitting stories comes into play. At every opportunity, the Product Owner and Developers should be aggressively trying to break stories down into the smallest possible item that will still deliver value. If no value is being delivered by a particular split, you are likely looking at tasks rather than separate Backlog Items. Every split

80

should be a vertical slice of functionality where possible. There is no value in delivering a UI that has no functionality behind it, for example.

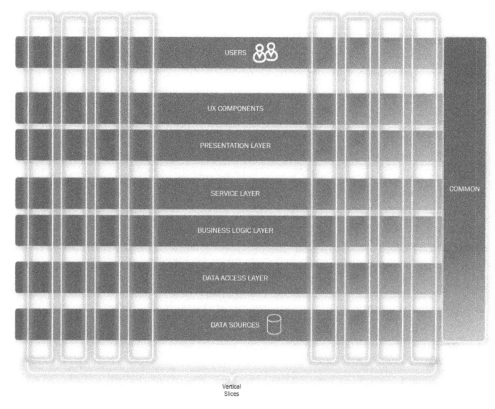

Figure 17 - Thin vertical slices of functionality

As Backlog Items are split, their order might change as work is negotiated and re-prioritized. Often there will be feedback from the Developers to the Product Owner that can be taken back to stakeholders. Additional clarification might be required before work can commence, or there might be an impediment to delivering a feature that the stakeholders need to be made aware of. This communication from the Product Owner back to stakeholders is one of the reasons we try to work a couple of Sprints ahead, so there is time to resolve issues before the Developers commit to working on the Backlog Item.

A well-refined Backlog Item will typically have certain characteristics:

- The business value of the story is clearly laid out.

- There is enough of a description of what is needed for the Developers to understand the work.
- Any dependencies should be identified and spelled out.
- The team has the skills to complete the work without outside assistance (or will be acquiring those skills).
- The acceptance criteria or conditions of satisfaction are clear and are testable.
- Any performance criteria already known should be articulated.
- The size of the Product Backlog Item has been estimated by the Developers.

Acceptance criteria should be clearly laid out for each Product Backlog Item and act as confirmation for that item. This communicates very precisely to the team what the Product Owner is looking for in order to know that the item is, in fact, Done. These will often be used by the QE Team as a basis to write test cases. The Product Owner may write the acceptance criteria herself or may collaborate with the Developers during Backlog Refinement to make sure everyone is on the same page. There should be no question as to exactly what constitutes proof that the item has been completed successfully.

Having a clean, well-refined Product Backlog makes it possible for Sprint Planning to take place efficiently. The Developers can now easily pick fully ready Backlog Items from the top of the Product Backlog, in accordance with their Sprint Goal. This is another opportunity to have a conversation about the work before starting, learn what might have changed since refinement, and add additional clarity to the card as needed. The team should verify that they still believe their initial estimate to be true or re-estimate if new information has come to light since refinement.

GOOOOOOOOOAL!

Sprint Goal

During Sprint Planning, the Developers should be asking -- and answering -- the following question:

"Why have you put these exact items into the Sprint Backlog, and not another group of items?"

The answer to this question is the Sprint Goal.

The Sprint Goal isn't simply "do all the things we pulled into the Sprint," or a list of all the PBIs the team has agreed upon, but it's a statement of purpose. It tells us what value we are adding during this increment, as detailed by the specific work we are doing. The Sprint Goal is not part of the 3-5-3 structure of Scrum, but it's an important statement that provides guidance to the Sprint.

During the Daily Scrum, we should always be checking the work we are doing against the Sprint Goal to make sure we are on track. The exact work the Developers are doing may change as details emerge, but as long as we are still on track to meet the Sprint Goal, the Sprint is doing just fine. The Developers should be negotiating specific work items with the Product Owner if needed to keep the Sprint Goal a valid one and make sure that the Sprint is a successful one.

The Sprint Goal shouldn't be so large and vague that it can't be realistically met. We still want to create SMART goals. Having multiple Sprint Goals can also create confusion. Which goal is more important? Is it okay for me to work on the second goal if there's nothing relating to the first one that I want to do right now? Keep it simple. Trying to make the Sprint Goal complicated or overly detailed will ultimately set the team up for failure. During Sprint Planning, ask the team, "How will we know when we have achieved our Sprint Goal?" If you are met with silence and looks of bewilderment, it's a good time to keep talking about the Goal.

Your Sprint Goal should be written out and on display for all to see. Write it out where you have your Daily Scrum meetings so the team can focus on it. Make it big and bold and immediately noticeable by everyone who walks past. There should never be an excuse for the team to lose sight of the Sprint Goal. Remind the team that there is no partial credit toward hitting the Sprint Goal. It's a simple, binary, pass/fail accomplishment. They either make it or they do not.

Product Goals

The Product Goal is part of the Product Backlog and describes some sort of future state for the product as a whole that the Scrum Team is working toward as a unit. As the Product Owner is creating Epics, Features and PBIs in the Product Backlog, it is with this future state in mind. The Product Backlog should then become emergent in nature as we strive toward this goal.

"A product is a vehicle to deliver value. It has a clear boundary, known stakeholders, well-defined users or customers. A product could be a service, a physical product, or something more abstract."

We can absolutely have multiple Product Goals, but it is important that we complete one goal before moving on to the next one. As a Scrum Team, it's entirely possible that our major releases are based around these Goals.

Stretch Goals

In the spirit of "under-commit, over-deliver" many teams will take on stretch goals as part of their Sprint, with an eye toward completing them if there is time remaining in the Sprint. Even under the best of circumstances, it's very difficult for the Developers to accurately take on exactly the right amount of work for a Sprint. We can know the team's velocity and accurately predict how much can be done, but there are any number of variables that can cause this forecast to vary. The idea of a stretch goal is to have something the Developers can push toward if the Sprint goes well. Before taking on a stretch goal, consider the following:

Is it better to:
1. Add work to a Sprint to make sure everyone always has something to do, even if that's outside the Sprint Goal?

2. Have team members be idle at the end of the Sprint if there is truly nothing that they can work on but the Sprint Goal is not at risk?

A challenging question but an important one. The answer, of course, is it varies. It's important to make sure that everyone knows that a stretch goal is not a commitment, it's not even in the forecast. It's something that the team <u>might</u> get to if they have time. The team needs to know that they aren't obligated to deliver on a stretch goal, and the business needs to understand that they cannot count on it being done in the Sprint.

For some teams, a stretch goal can be a great thing. They like the challenge of having something extra to work toward, and they will aggressively try to get there, with the safety of not being on the hook if they can't quite make it. For these teams, it's good to give them something to push their limits, while making sure they understand it is work that only can be touched once the Sprint Goal has been met.

For other teams, stretch goals are a disaster in the making. They see everything in the Sprint Backlog as a commitment and try to overdo it. This becomes an amount of work that crushes the team under its weight. I have seen team members skip ahead to a stretch goal Product Backlog Item because it is easier than work that is in alignment with the actual Sprint Goal. When this happens, the Sprint Goal immediately becomes at risk, because Developers are working on the wrong things and value is not being created and delivered.

I specifically asked about stretch goals during one training class I had and was told "NO." We either forecast the work or we don't. There is nothing in between. This fell into the camp that it's better to have idle team members and make sure the Sprint Goal is never at risk. I can appreciate this. It feels wrong to have people with "nothing to do," but it's more important that we successfully deliver value in every Sprint. The decision about how to tackle stretch goals is something you should discuss with your team and let them make the right decision.

We Missed the Shot, Now What?

There's a great blog post by Mike Cohn[xiii] about why it's okay to not always get everything done every single time. He likens it to a basketball player -- you take the shot when you have it, even knowing that sometimes you're going to miss. But we can't let the fear of missing the shot prevent us from even taking it in the first place.

The best basketball players are only going to make half their shots (free throws notwithstanding). The best baseball players are going to get an out 70% of the time they are at bat. The best Scrum Teams will not always finish everything in their forecast every single time. We don't know what we don't know, and many times work will emerge in the middle of the Sprint that will cause our initial estimates to be very, very wrong. That's normal and should be expected when we are doing complex work.

We embrace built-in instability when we become Agile. We minimize the risk of throwaway work by running in short cycles, but there is always a chance that something has changed and we will need to rapidly inspect and adapt. There will be Sprints where the Developers do not hit their forecast as planned due to unforeseen reasons. This could be anything from a change in requirements, unexpected work in the form of defects, or just that the work took longer than anyone original anticipated. All of these things are normal and will happen to the team on a regular basis. If a team is meeting its forecast the majority of the time, with the occasional miss, there is nothing to worry about, and this is a sign of a healthy team.

What's important is that the Developers are always focused on the Sprint Goal. Work can be moved into or out of the Sprint at any time if the Developers and Product Owner agree, but the Sprint Goal should still be intact and valid. If we hit the Sprint Goal, even if we have drastically reduced the number of PBIs or velocity of the team to get there, the Sprint was a success.

But what happens if the Sprint Goal is compromised and is no longer viable? There are two options at play here. The first and most radical is to immediately cancel the Sprint and start a new one, keeping all Events for ending and starting a Sprint intact. This should only be done in the direst of circumstances as it will impact the entire Scrum Team in a very real way. The Product Owner makes the ultimate decision to cancel a Sprint, often with advice from stakeholders, the Scrum Master, the Developers or any combination of these. Expect resources to be consumed as everything restarts, and the team will take a hit in time, energy, and motivation.

Less impactful is to see if there's a way to negotiate the Sprint Goal to see what part of it <u>can</u> be met, and to negotiate the work within the Sprint to meet the adjusted goal. While this may still result in some throwaway work, the overall impact on the Scrum Team will be greatly lessened. An open dialogue between the Product Owner and the Developers is crucial when the Sprint Goal is in jeopardy.

Cancelling a Sprint is an extreme and potentially traumatic event that should only be used with extreme caution. I'm fond of saying that everything we are doing is written down in wet sand, and the tide is coming in. Keep that in mind as you progress through your Sprints, and you will meet your Goal 80% of the time, if not more.

VI - In My Estimation...

Hours, Story Points, and the Paradox of Estimating

There are some things that are really easy to agree on when it comes to estimating:

- Estimating is important.
- Estimating is hard.
- Estimates are always wrong.

Of course, there are some fundamental problems with how we estimate. Traditionally, the question we are asked when it's time to estimate effort is "How long will this take?" If you're still asking this question, I respectfully suggest you're doing it wrong. In fact, you couldn't be doing it more wrong. Study after study has shown that estimating complex work in hours (or any time-based unit) is the worst way to approach it. In fact, you might be better off not estimating at all than to take a SWAG at how many hours something will take.

Why is this?

The truth is that estimating in hours or days actually creates a losing situation for everyone involved. To start, the second you provide that estimate you've essentially signed a contract that says "I will do this in a fixed amount of time." That's not what you meant to do, of course, but that's almost invariably what happens. There are now three things that can happen:

- We hit our estimate exactly. This actually never happens, but I suppose it's possible, so I will leave it here.
- The work takes significantly less time than expected.
- The work takes significantly longer than expected.

Starting at the bottom, when something takes longer than expected this leaves us feeling like something is wrong. This work should be easier and it should only take so long; the problem must be that I am not as good at my job as I thought. Get caught in this trap and the thing that is already 'late' starts to fall further behind as you begin to question yourself about everything you do. It's pretty clear why this is bad.

But when we take less time, that's not bad, right? Guess again. There are two common scenarios here too, neither of which are good. The first is that we can find ourselves wondering what we missed and start to second guess ourselves. We start reviewing every line of code and looking for the obvious mistake that we didn't account for and start to gold-plate the work that is perfectly fine! The other thing I have personally seen is that we leave a User Story marked open with some hours left, and when another one runs longer people start "working" on the completed item to steal away a few hours so that they stay on track and their burndown looks good. Never mind transparency, it's about making sure we don't look bad.

We suck at precise estimates. Don't let anyone try to convince you otherwise. We are, however, really good at judging if Thing A is larger or smaller than Thing B. Or at least we're reasonably better at it, which is close enough.

Figure 18 - Planning Poker Cards

Story Points have become widely accepted because it gives us a way to estimate and remove time from the equation. If Thing A is three points and Thing B feels slightly larger, it's likely five points. We're good. How long will a 3-point story take? I have absolutely no idea. The size of a story and how long it will take to complete have no relationship to each other. Even in a world where we could easily make that determination, it would vary from team to team. Team A's idea of a 5-point story might only be a 2-point story to Team B. And that's all totally okay. There is no way to compare estimates across teams, and don't get sucked into that trap.

The great paradox of estimating is that the more imprecise our estimates are, they more accurate they actually become. Story Points give us that sweet spot of imprecision. It is enough to just know that Backlog Item 1 is bigger than Backlog Item 2, and that it will fit into the bucket of a certain number of Story Points. That is literally all we need to know. We can reliably say that a 3-point story is approximately 3x larger than a 1-point story, though.

It's important when we estimate that we are looking at our DoD and sizing the entire Backlog Item from when we start to when we are done. We don't add up "developer points," "testing points," and "deployment points," and arrive at a final estimate. Instead, we consider the entire body of work involved and think about the effort as a whole. When not sure how big something is, err on the side of caution and allow yourself to be persuaded otherwise. (But be prepared to defend your estimate!)

Teaching our teams to estimate using Story Points instead of hours is not always easy. We naturally want to think of things in terms of how long it will take. I use the analogy of a marathon when I talk about how big a story is. I know a marathon is 26.2 "story points." How long it takes is widely variable. An elite runner is going to complete the marathon in a little over two hours, whereas it would take an average runner twice that time. The amount of work was identical (26.2 miles), but the time it took was vastly different. It's still a 26.2-point story no matter how long it takes to complete. There is no correlation of hours to Story Points. Every developer -- and therefore every team -- works at a different pace. Work that might take Pradip 12 hours to complete might only require 5 hours from Christine, but they both agree it's a two-point story based on what they know. If the story revolves around creating middleware, which is Christine's specialty, this is absolutely to be expected. The amount of work is still the same, it's just that Christine has an easier time of it than Pradip would, because his deep specialty lies elsewhere.

There is a sense in certain circles that "one point = one person-day" and it should be easy to extrapolate an estimate based on that. The problem becomes that the Developers will then shy away from estimating in points and will automatically think of "It will take me x hours," and make that conversion. Looking back, this might make Christine estimate the item as a one-point story, while Pradip might now make it a three, because he is conservative outside of his area of expertise. While this isn't necessarily bad, our estimates should be developer neutral. We don't know who is going to be working on a Backlog Item at the time we estimate it, and our estimate in Story Points should reflect that element of neutrality.

Remember that estimates are always wrong. An otherwise meaningless number that says "This is bigger than that" is really all we need to know. Given enough time estimating this way rather than using hours to load up to exactly how much time in in a Sprint, we will get a clearer picture of how much work a team can accomplish, and they will actually go faster and with higher quality.

I use a game to coach my teams through improving how they estimate.

The Sizing Game

I love games, and I use games for many things. I blame my past life as a Cub Scout leader for teaching me how to make up games on the fly. Feel free to steal and modify my idea if it makes sense for you.

Story Points don't inherently make sense to people. I was met with no small amount of
resistance when I first mentioned using them recently. I decided to start with something that does make sense, and we talked about t-shirt sizes. Easy. Everyone has worn a t-shirt at some point.

We started with a simple scale of sizes (S, M, L, XL, 2X) and some ground rules. The team has 30 seconds per estimate to decide how big something is, and a consensus is not required. Majority opinion is fine.

First up: I ask my teams to tell me what MY t-shirt size is. My actual size is irrelevant. I don't care if they decide I am wearing a shirt the size of a circus tent. Having a thick skin and a sense of humor is an important skill as a Scrum Master, by the way. I write my name on the board beneath whatever size they give me.

The important thing is that I am now officially a reference story. And that reference story is something they know, not an intangible something. Now that I am established, the real game can begin. My mind works in silly ways, so I latched onto the term "relative sizing" and decided to size my relatives.

With that in mind, I show the team a photo of myself with my younger son. What's *his* t-shirt size? My son is taller and leaner than I am. A lot taller and leaner, actually, because he's young and in shape. The photo I use was taken the day he graduated from US Army Basic Training, in fact. Does his added height put him in a larger shirt, or does the fact that he doesn't have the dad bod put him in a smaller size? Once again... the truth doesn't really matter; whatever the team decides is perfectly correct. His name is now added to the board.

Next up? Here's another picture of my son with two of his best friends. His friends, of course, are not close to the same size he is. One is far shorter and one carries more muscle mass. Because chances are the team has different sizes for my son and me, this now gives them two points of reference going forward. Names added once again.

One more picture. My son with my sister and my brother-in-law. My sister is several inches shorter than I am, and my brother-in-law is built like a college football lineman (which, in fact, he was). By now the estimates are all over the map, and we have a set of six names on the board that have been sized.

It's now time to blow up the scale. To this mix of people, I add two more outside my personal circle of family and friends:

- Peter Dinklage
- Andre the Giant

Every time the photo of Andre appears when I run this game, the room is laughing. How do you possibly guess what size t-shirt Andre the Giant wore? And yet we find a way to expand the top end of the scale and arrive at an answer.

The scale of sizes has now changed from where we started. We often have an XS at the bottom and an XXXXL (the actual number of X's may vary) at the top. At this point, I start putting story point numbers alongside the t-shirt sizes (1,2,3,5,8,13,20,40,100) and the teams can begin to see how just thinking about the size of something translates easily into story points.

The beauty in all of it is that none of the estimates need to be correct. In fact, they are usually way off, but that's totally okay. The team's perception of the size of the work is all that counts, and those estimates are good enough. What one team decides will almost certainly not align with what another team decides, and that's perfectly great too!

The same rule applies when we start estimating our actual User Stories. We don't need to be perfect; we just need to be close enough and agree on what a certain number of points means, relatively speaking.

What about Tasks?

It's important that we keep close track of our PBIs and bugs, and that we have estimated the effort for each. It's also important - especially when the Developers are swarming around work - that items have been broken down into easily digested tasks. Is it important that we estimate those tasks, though?

My definitive answer here is maybe.

Tasks tend to not be tracked using Story Points but in hours, which is less than optimal. Using hours on tasks and tracking remaining work does help to feed your burndown chart, if such a thing is important to you. If the digital tool you are using requires hours and you need a chart, then you might find great importance in having all of the tasks associated with a given Backlog Item estimated.

I would, however, argue against doing so. Tasks are small parts of a larger PBI and do not actually deliver value on their own. If the task delivers value, shouldn't it have been broken out into a separate PBI? If we have half the tasks done on a PBI, we are not done. No value has been created or delivered, and there is still work to do before the team can realize the points associated with that Backlog Item. It should go without saying that we don't assign credit for undone work, so we don't burn down some random portion of the story points assigned based on being partway to Done. Estimating tasks is a level of granularity that is not needed to get our work to Done.

The added level of detail that is gained from estimating down to the task level is minimal, and the accuracy actually decreases as you get more and more granular. The sweet spot is finding where you have just the right amount of detail, and that spot is invariably at the Product Backlog Item level. Estimating in tasks - particularly if those estimates are in hours - makes our estimates increasingly meaningless. The other bad part of estimating in hours is that it becomes far too easy for someone to simply add up the hours and say, "Well, clearly if is a three-point story and it should take 18 hours, I can now extrapolate that every story point is six hours and I know exactly how long all the work will take!" Don't fall into this trap as only bad things can happen here.

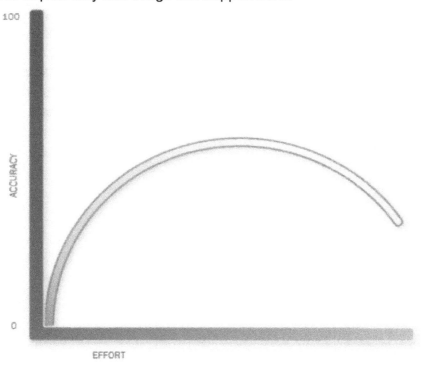

Figure 19 - Estimation Effort and Diminishing Returns

Again, I can see where it might be needed. I've worked with tools that only generated a burn-down chart based on tasks which had to be estimated in hours, regardless of how the parent Product Backlog Item was being estimated. I've also seen where throwing out those estimates and focusing on getting the PBI to Done was the only thing that mattered. Tasks are incredibly useful for breaking down the work, particularly when multiple developers are swarming around a single PBI. Spending time guessing at how much time each task will take is largely time wasted. Split the story if the task is delivering value on its own, or focus on the entire PBI, and you will have exactly the right amount of detail in your estimates.

Inside the Matrix

Learning how to estimate well is hard and it takes practice. Teams not used to estimating in Story Points will have a difficult time making the adjustment. The most common problem is trying to figure out how many hours one story point is worth and trying to draw some equivalency there. I have had great success using a matrix to assist my teams with how to do initial estimates. It's by no means perfect, but it can provide a starting point for newer teams as to how to reasonably arrive at a consensus in their estimates.

ESTIMATING MATRIX					
A m w t o r o k f	XL	5	8	13	20
	L	3	5	8	13
	M	2	3	5	8
	S	1	2	3	5
		S	M	L	XL
		Complexity			

Figure 20 - The Estimating Matrix

The matrix itself is very simple, only requiring two inputs. The members of the team should be only thinking about the amount of work involved and the complexity of that work. How long the actual work will take is irrelevant. Each Developer should consider whether these things are Small, Medium, Large or eXtra Large and then crosstab to arrive at a baseline estimate for the work.

For example: The team needs to go through the project and change the endpoints currently being used to a new one published by another team. The existing endpoints are used frequently and there are many of them to be changed. The team estimates that this work is not complex at all (S) but would require a significant amount of work to make sure all endpoints are correctly changed and completely tested (L). Based on this, the team agrees that this is a three-point story.

The team has to write a new class to transform incoming data from an endpoint into a feed which is going to be published to many, widely distributed client locations. The team agrees that this won't require a lot of work (S), but it will be quite complex to make this change (XL). From here, the team agrees that this is a five-point story.

As we play Planning Poker, each Developer considers these factors on his/her own and votes based on that understanding. Then the team discusses the outlier votes and we re-vote until we have consensus. Using the matrix gives individual team members quick talking points to explain how they reached their estimate.

You will notice also that areas of the matrix are shaded. The lighter the color, the better. Any items that are falling into the five or eight-point buckets may need additional splitting or are likely to require swarming to make sure they are completed within the Sprint. The shorter your Sprints are, the more important this becomes. Anything that is a 13 or 20-point story is generally considered too large, needs additional discussion and should definitely be split. Using this method also lets us pull the larger 40 and 100-point cards out of the deck when playing Planning Poker. These cards are very useful when we are talking about features early on (which we might just be putting vague t-shirt sizes on anyway), but anything that big during Backlog Refinement or Sprint Planning is clearly too large to work on and is going to require additional attention before it is ready for the Developers to bring into their Sprint Backlog.

This matrix isn't for everyone. Mature teams won't need any assistance getting estimates done and will be confident in their ability to quickly size a Backlog Item.

The Myth of Velocity

Effectively estimating work (preferably in Story Points) allows us to get a picture of how much work a team can pull in any given Sprint. This is the team's velocity; how fast they are going in SP/S (Story Points per Sprint). Velocity is absolutely an important metric and we should be using it. Like any metric, it's easy to misuse or abuse and wind up with something that is contrary to what is important.

At its core, all velocity does is tell us how fast the team is going. Nothing more, nothing less. During Sprint Planning, we can use the team's current historical velocity -- typically an average of their last three to six sprints -- to predict the amount of work they can achieve. The Scrum Master should serve as a check to make sure the team doesn't overburden themselves with work that is not likely to get to Done. This is an excellent use of velocity and should be encouraged among your teams.

The problem with velocity is two-fold. One, there is a tendency to feel that we need to always push to do more in every Sprint; two, there is a sense that we should be able to compare velocity across teams to determine which teams are performing best. These are both inherently wrong.

The idea of getting the team to go faster is a natural one and one that a Product Owner is likely to push hard for. We naturally want to see the team deliver even more value in a short period of time. Telling the team that they can do 50 points of work when they are historically doing 30 is only going to set them up for failure and frustration, however. I have always maintained that it is better to under-commit and over-deliver. If Team PAWS is doing 30 points historically, give them a buffer and only let them load up 25 points in the Sprint. The first couple of Sprints, this might be all they get done. Over time, as good Scrum practices take hold, the team will find themselves finishing that 25 points earlier in the Sprint and looking to the Product Backlog to see if there is anything else that they can get to Done within the remaining days of a Sprint. This will just happen naturally as your Developers mature. This is how we increase velocity. You should see a slow and steady climb toward the team's peak performance. There's no magic trick to make it happen, and you can't force it to happen before the team is ready. Telling the team to just do more points will often simply lead to the team padding their estimates to attain higher numbers with the same amount of work. All that is required is a steady hand and patience, and the team will surprise you with how much faster they get. The focus should not be on raw output but on outcomes. If the Sprint Goal was met, it does not matter how many points the team got done; the Sprint was a success. Conversely, if Team PAWS delivers 50 points of work, but they have completely missed the Sprint Goal, what value was gained by the extra velocity?

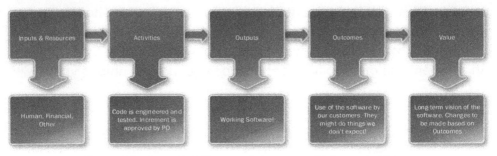

Figure 21 - Outputs influence Outcomes, which create Value

If the team makes it a goal of theirs to increase their velocity, do it a little at a time rather than trying to make a dramatic leap. Large jumps will tend to lead to large amounts of work carrying over from one Sprint to another on a regular basis. We don't want this to happen. Teams will have this problem often as they are maturing, and you will see Sprints with a low velocity followed by a Sprint with an exceptional velocity. This is one of the biggest reasons to use a rolling average of the velocity from the previous three Sprints as your team's current velocity to even out any such spikes. Let the team take on a Kaizen to improve their velocity but temper it with reality. Let them see their historical data and allow them to judge how much faster they can realistically get without bloating their estimates.

One of the tricks to increasing velocity is to get work done earlier in the Sprint. Obviously, if everything is code complete on the last day of the Sprint, there will not be sufficient time to test everything and get it Done (in accordance with your DoD, of course). There are several ways to do this: work more hours, start earlier, add more people. None of these necessarily solve your problem. Purely working more hours will quickly lead to team burnout. Starting earlier is essentially saying "Make our Sprints longer or let us carry things over," neither of which solves the problem, and adding people risks invoking Brooks' Law. There's a simpler way to get work done faster and earlier in each Sprint. Do smaller things. As we've seen when talking about Planning and Estimating, we ideally want to break our work down into the smallest possible pieces that each deliver value. By spending the necessary time to do this, we give ourselves the best possible chance to deliver that

100

value quickly in each Sprint, and that will in turn lead to increased velocity.

I've seen this in action with a team I worked with recently. When I joined the team, they were doing three-week Sprints, and there was no real sense of what a relatively-sized story point was. After a little coaching, we made the decision to move to two-week Sprints, releasing approximately every two Sprints. As expected, we slowed down…briefly. Within a few months of this new cadence, we were releasing 2.5 times the value, in just a week's more time. It works, but we have to allow for discomfort, and trust that we can get there. The Developers will surprise you with their ability to effect change rapidly.

As for comparing velocity across teams? Just don't do it. Ever. I get it. We want to have a meaningful way to see which teams are over-performing and which teams are underperforming. The problem is that velocity is not that metric. If every team estimated every PBI and every bug exactly the same way every time, were all exactly the same size and had exactly the same skill sets, we could maybe use velocity as a cross team metric. The reality is that these conditions simply do not exist. What one team estimates as a five-point story will be a two-point story to another team and an eight-point story to a third. None of these estimates are wrong, they are simply how that team views the work in front of them. Teams are not all the same size at all times, people come and go, teams form and disband according to the needs of the business, and we count on that built-in instability. Because teams are self-organizing and self-managing, they have the skills they need for what they are working on, which is likely different from every other team in your organization. This too is normal and natural. We rely on these things for Scrum to succeed.

If Team A is doing 50 points of work and Team B is "only" doing 30 points, that doesn't automatically make Team A superior. They might have a larger team, they might estimate more conservatively, they might have a greater degree of automation in place, they might be more mature, they might simply be better at splitting stories into smaller chunks and getting more done that way. There are so many variables that go into a team's velocity that it is truly impossible to compare.

Burn, Baby, Burn

My Love/Hate Relationship with Sprint Burndowns

I admit to mixed feelings about Sprint burndowns. Many teams use them as part of their big visible display to show progress toward the team's goals for a Sprint, and they've become a standard part of the toolkit. Think back to the 3-5-3 structure, however, and you will recall that the burndown is not one of the three artifacts of Scrum and is not actually required for you to make Scrum work. The Scrum Guide mentions burndowns only in passing along with other practices of monitoring progress. It also explicitly states that none of these practices replaces Empiricism. An old version of the Scrum Guide did mandate a burndown chart, but this has long since gone away. Yet the practice of requiring a burndown, often in hours, still is widely accepted.

In theory, Sprint burndowns are useful. A good burndown provides a quick at a glance view of how the team is progressing toward their goal and shows where things might be tracking behind and adjustments might need to be made within the Sprint. Sounds awesome, right?

Sure. But does it really work that way? My experience is that it really doesn't, and so that's about where my personal tolerance for burndowns ends. I recognize that for others the burndown is awesome. Your team might do well with a Sprint burndown or your organization might require them, in which case you should absolutely be using them to your full advantage.

The reality of every Sprint, of course, is that work changes as we learn things. User Stories may be moved in or out of the Sprint, and tasks will be changed as we go. Particularly in the first few days of a Sprint, the burndown is more likely to look like a child's drawing of mountains than an actual burndown. If a Scrum Team successfully identifies ALL work in the Sprint up front, along with every task (correctly estimated), and nothing changes whatsoever, then yes, the burndown is neat.

When was the last time this happened? I can honestly say "I don't remember this ever happening." New work is always being discovered, defects are being found as QE starts testing the functionality being added to User Stories, and the Sprint Backlog is a living artifact of work. If the Sprint Backlog is written in stone on Day One of the Sprint, there's probably something going on that the Scrum Team is missing.

In fact, I have only ever seen perfectly clean burndown charts once, and that was when everyone was just making it up and burning hours off tasks at random to account for a full day's worth of work at 100% utilization. If you don't know why that is bad, refer back to the very first chapter!

From that, you might guess that I'm not exactly a fan of the burndown chart. I might have been overheard several times saying "I don't care about the burndown." They're mildly interesting at best (to me). Most of the time, I ignore them completely. I'm more interested in the discussion the Developers are having about their progress toward meeting their Sprint Goal than what the burndown chart looks like. Toward the end of a Sprint, the burndown starts to gain importance as it provides a clearer picture of how close the Developers are toward the ultimate goal of a working increment of Done software, but even then it's not the tell-all.

The true story lies within what the Developers are talking about during their Daily Scrum and the conversations they are having with the Product Owner about moving toward Done. Actively listening during these conversations will answer your questions far better than a burndown chart ever could.

I am also not a huge fan, as you will recall, of estimating tasks -- seeing it largely as time wasted. If precise task estimates are what is driving your burndown chart, your options here might be limited. Don't let the tool you are using dictate what the correct practices are for your team, however. What works best for your team should always take precedence over a chart generated by a digital tool.

Having said that, there is always still a way to maintain your burndown. I've had success using two different approaches when I have needed to keep the burndown up to date. Both required a little creativity but accomplished the ultimate goal.

The first and most obvious one is to generate the burndown against the Story Points for entire PBIs. As they are moved to Done, we burn down that many points. If your tool doesn't allow you to do this, don't be afraid to grab the markers and draw your own burndown on a whiteboard or easel pad. Even a roughly drawn burndown chart can be better than none and will accurately reflect how the team is progressing toward Done work.

The alternate approach when you absolutely must use the digital tool and tasks is simply to set the effort required for every task to one. The tasks become binary; either they are Done or they are not. When individual tasks are done, burn the one down to zero. It's not perfect, but it will allow the tool a way to create its burndown without you having to worry about whether they are perfectly estimated.

Don't focus on the pretty chart. Focus on what the Developers are saying and you'll find you have the best information possible.

Burn it Up

My mixed feelings about Sprint burndowns doesn't mean I disregard all burndown or burnup charts altogether. In fact, one of my favorite tools is a release burnup chart. When working on a new product or a major enhancement to an existing product that will require several sprints worth of work to deliver in full, this is easily my favorite way of tracking progress toward that release. It's worth pointing out before I go into detail that burnups, like burndowns, are not actually part of Scrum but are potential tools to monitor progress toward goals.

The chart I use looks something like this:

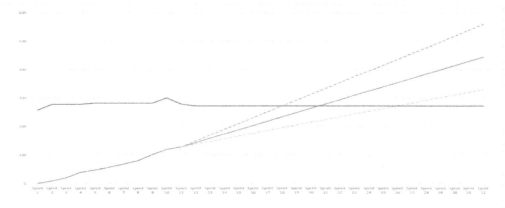

Figure 22 - A sample Release Burnup with the Cone of Uncertainty

As you can see from this, it's not overly complicated and only requires a few points of input to track. The team's velocity per sprint drives the primary line on the chart, showing us the exact history of our progress toward a goal. That goal is represented by the horizontal line. You'll see where that line has moved over time as work comes into the Product Backlog or is moved out of scope. Our target shifts and it's important that we keep track of that. The center trend line tracks ahead using the previous three sprints worth of velocity data to determine the team's average velocity, and we build our cone of uncertainty using the standard deviation for the same three sprints. This gives us a picture of when we think we will cross the finish line and how we might trend faster or slower as we move out into the future.

It's a simple but powerful picture.

At a quick glance we can determine two important things about our product:
- The stability of the Product Backlog
- In which Sprint we expect to be complete and ready for release

The business and our customers always want to know when we are going to deliver the important work they are asking for. This gives us a quick way to forecast that data, using the empirical evidence of what the team has been able to deliver and what we know about our Product Backlog.

105

We can also see where there is major churn in the Product Backlog. It's important for us to be able to shine a light on when the scope drastically increased or when we moved items out of the backlog to help us get to being complete that much sooner. There are a lot of metrics we can use, but this simple chart gives one of the clearest pictures of the forecast that we have.

If You Choose Not to Decide

I would be remiss if I didn't talk about an entirely different philosophy here. What happens if we don't bother to estimate at all? There is a case to be made for completely forgoing estimates, and you'll remember in Chapter II where I talked about my team doing exactly that. There is certainly a case to be made for eliminating estimates completely. Having done both, I am increasingly in the #NoEstimates camp.

Just as I stated that time spent estimating tasks is time wasted and better used on developing software, so goes the case for not estimating. Let the team simply decide what they can get done in a Sprint and let them get to it. If you are like me and are not a fan of the Sprint burn-down chart, this aligns very nicely. You can't burn down what you don't have a size for. Work is simply binary -- it's Done or it's not. Period.

The Scrum Guide is completely silent on the practice of estimating, stating only that the Developers are responsible for all estimates. This would automatically include the choice to not estimate at all. While many Scrum courses will teach estimating and Planning Poker, this is not actually a part of the framework and is just a practice that has evolved over time. Many, myself included, would make the case that it's a great practice if you choose to estimate. What's really important here, however, is that it might not be the ideal practice for your team. The most important thing is that you know how your team works and how your organization works, and make the correct decision based on your needs.

If you need a way to track progress toward a release or to track the burndown during a Sprint, you will require estimates. If getting the team to spend the maximum time on writing code and less time in Backlog

Refinement and Sprint Planning is critical, you might be able to forego estimates. You may find that only large PBIs require estimating, and smaller, more trivial work, does not require the added attention of sizing it. Even if you choose not to estimate, there may be times when it is unavoidable. How often have we all been asked by the business when we anticipate completion of a project? It happens all of the time, and you will need a way to provide a meaningful answer. You will be forced to make some kind of estimates on the work you know and SWAG the work you don't.

So here's the big question: What value do you gain by estimating? Velocity? Sure, but you can get a sense of that based purely on the range of PBIs your team can typically accomplish in a Sprint. Knowing your cycle times further allows you to create an SLA, where you can say "We will deliver 90% of work within 4 business days." Pretty good stuff. The other arguments for estimating fall out the same way. There's a valid counterargument for #NoEstimates. All we care about is how much work we can get done. Period. We already know we aren't showing incomplete work in the Sprint Review, so that aligns. We know we don't want our leadership trying to compare velocities across teams, so don't give them one!

All that said, even now there are times when I want my teams to estimate. If we are tackling new, challenging work that I want the Developers to really think about, I might ask them for estimates up front. Not so much for the actual number, but more to get them engaged and really thinking deeply about the problem we are trying to solve. The number might be one I don't care about, but there is sometimes value in the process of getting the Developers to really think through potential paths forward.

As with everything else we do in Scrum, the important thing is whether we are delivering value. If estimates are not providing value to your team or organization, you might be perfectly fine with not estimating and getting the team to coding that much faster. Know your environment and make the correct decision for you.

VII - Retrospectively Speaking

Retrospective 101

The Retrospective Prime Directive

"Regardless of what we discover, we understand and truly believe that everyone did the best job they could, given what they knew at the time, their skills and abilities, the resources available, and the situation at hand."[xiv]

Let me just say this up front:
I love Sprint Retrospectives.

The Retrospective is easily my favorite event in Scrum. It's also the hardest one to get just exactly perfect. I make no claim to having done this – there is always room to improve, after all – but I try very hard to get as close as I can. There was a period over two years where I never repeated a Sprint Retrospective activity for a team, and my teams were always eager to see what new madness I had in store for them at the end of the Sprint.

If you haven't read <u>Agile Retrospectives: Making Good Teams Great</u> by Esther Derby and Diana Larsen yet, go order your copy right now. This book will teach you far more about Retrospectives than anything else. Many of the sites you find online borrow directly from this outstanding source material. To cover the basics; regardless of the activity we choose in any given Sprint Retrospective, there are always a set of Inputs, Outputs, and an activity flow that we should strive to follow.

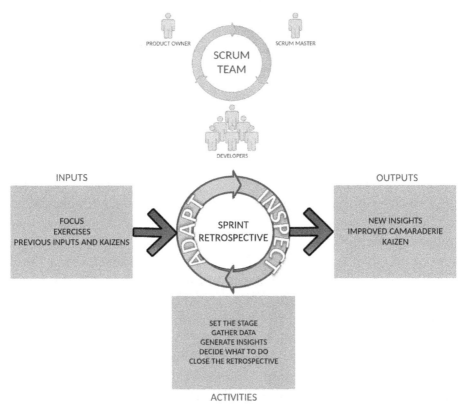

Figure 23 - The Sprint Retrospective

Going into a Sprint Retrospective we need a couple of things: Focus (this is a no laptops, no phones event), the Exercise(s) we are going to be doing, and any Insights gained during the Sprint. In addition, if this is not your first Sprint Retrospective, bring a list of all the Kaizens the team chose during the previous Retrospective. Make those Kaizens visible to the team and ask how we did on achieving them.

The Retrospective itself takes a certain form with five basic steps:
- Set the Stage
- Gather Data
- Generate Insights
- Decide What to Do
- Close the Retrospective

Setting the stage can be as simple as asking everyone for one word describing how they feel about the Sprint. It can be running down the list of Kaizens and asking how we did. The idea is to start providing focus and set up a goal for the Retrospective. Welcome everyone and thank them for taking part. Get everyone to speak early when possible. Reiterate the Retrospective Prime Directive and make sure the team is comfortable with the fact that this is a safe event for them to talk about anything that is on their minds. Remind the team of the Sprint Values if that helps. Get everyone ready for what is to come next.

Gathering Data is where your chosen exercise for the Retrospective will take place. Whether you choose to go around the room and have team members speak one at a time, pass out sticky notes and have people writing down thoughts, or have a game planned to illustrate a point that you want to coach the team on, this is where it happens. Regardless of the exact format of your activity, it's important that the team's safety is taken into consideration and that every member of the Scrum Team has a chance to provide his or her thoughts. Everyone's input is important. While gathering data might not take up the largest portion of your Retrospective, it is a critical step. Without taking a few minutes to generate and gather data from the rest of the Scrum Team, no additional progress can be made.

Generating Insights is likely to be the part of your Retrospective that takes the most time. Here you will take the data that was gathered and analyze it as a team. Discuss your findings to see where there is a great deal of common ground and where there's an outlier that might need to be addressed. Remember here that silence is your friend, and you need to be prepared to let the room remain quiet if nobody is speaking. Don't provide insights on your own but allow the team to come up with what they see and what is important for them. Facilitate the discussion but don't steer it. Let the team surprise you.

Deciding what to do is perhaps the most important step. We can generate all of the data in the world and come up with brilliant insights, but if we don't choose actions to make the team better during the next Sprint, what was the point? Here again, it's imperative that the team drives this discussion. They are the ones who will be committing to an action in almost every case so don't choose something for them. Ask questions but allow the team to think and decide what steps they can take to make improvements, based on the data and insights they have gained. This Kaizen should then immediately go into the Sprint Backlog for the new Sprint so that the entire team sees it at all times. Don't try to do too many things at once. It's better to take one or two improvements and make them happen than to come up with several and fall short. Small incremental changes work best!

Close the Retrospective in any way you feel is appropriate. Recap the activity and actions. Get a one-word response from everyone on how they feel about the actions they have chosen. Ask how the team feels about how this Retrospective went and ask for feedback toward making future Retrospectives even better. How you close will vary from one Retrospective to the next, but do something to wrap up and indicate to the team that things are done. Be sure to thank the team for their time and their participation because without their input, nothing can get done. This is also an excellent chance to share kudos among the team for a job well done during the Sprint and recognize their hard work!

When you have all of these things accomplished, the team should leave with one or more action items, and they should feel empowered to make the improvements they committed to. There should be some new insights they have gained, and an open mind toward new insights for the coming Sprint. The Retrospective should provide closure to the Sprint and leave the entire Scrum Team in a place where they know that what they are doing together is working. Let the energy from your Retrospective carry into the new Sprint, and let the team know that they are capable of doing anything they set their minds to!

A Retrospective Toolkit

I am a big believer in games and any way to make an activity fun is always a winner for me. If I can use a game to teach a concept or to facilitate a discussion, I do so. My previous life as a Cub Scout leader taught me the power of a good game and how to always be ready to do something unexpected and silly. I will illustrate a couple of the activities I have run later in this chapter, but I encourage you to seek out other ideas online or to make up your own!

Over time I have built what I call my Retrospective Toolkit. My desk is never without these things, because I never know when I might need one or more of them. Here's what's in my toolkit and why they are in there.

Notebook
One of the most important tools I have is a simple spiral bound notebook. Any time I get an idea -- whether it's one from a book, something I found online, or something I made up -- I sketch it out in the notebook. Ideas I really like or that I found particularly fun and useful, I will go back and ink in using all of the colors I have at my disposal. I revisit the notebook constantly, looking for ideas I haven't used or drawing out rough sketches of new ideas I have. You don't need to be a great artist to draw in your notebook or on a whiteboard. Simple drawings that convey the point are often the best ones.

Here's an example of a page in my notebook right now. You can see where I sketched everything out in pencil early and went back and colored it in to make it stand out.

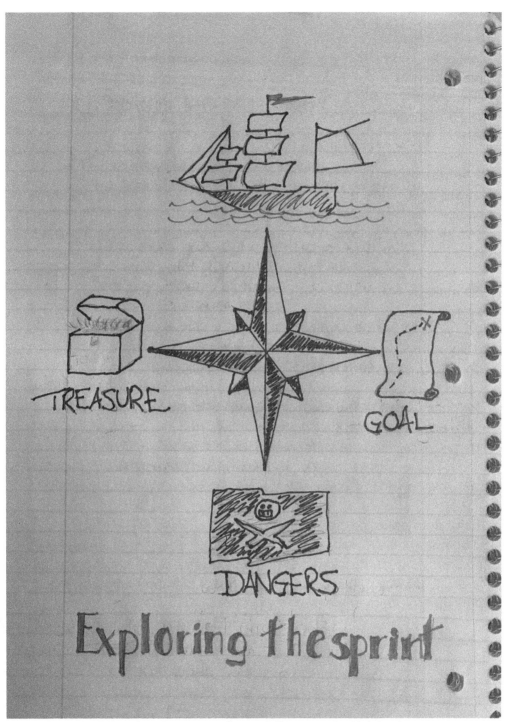

Figure 24 - Actual page from my Retrospective Notebook

Dry-erase paper

Most of the rooms in my office have whiteboard paint or have access to an actual whiteboard, but you never know when you might be stuck without one. Having a roll of this ready to go lets you turn any wall into a whiteboard wall. I don't need to use this often, but it's saved me more than once when I would have otherwise been stuck.

Dry-erase markers

You will never have enough of these, and you will want both broad and fine point markers. Get every color you can put your hands on and use them all. Don't be content with the basic red, blue, green, and black, but load up your color palette to its fullest potential. Adding color to your whiteboard helps make things stand out and using unusual colors will help make your Retrospectives stand apart from other meetings. Maximize your creativity!

Sticky notes

Every Scrum Master has piles of these. As with markers, don't be afraid to seek out lots of different colors and use them. Use colors to denote specific concepts; I always use green sticky notes for things that are positive and red/pink sticky notes for things that require attention, for example. Mix in colors to denote concepts you are trying to discuss and allow like colors to be quickly grouped. I burn through sticky notes like crazy and consider them one of the most important tools I have.

Sticky note easel pad

Sometimes you will want to take what you talk about in a Retrospective and bring it out of the room. Having easel-sized sticky notes gives you the ability to write things down, bring it out of the room and stick those notes up anywhere in the team's work area.

Pens

Because someone always forgets to bring one.

Permanent Markers

Less used than dry-erase markers by far, but I have colors of these to match every dry-erase marker in my toolkit. I will use these to write on sticky notes when I want to use a specific color to correspond to something I have written on the whiteboard. Again, your use of color helps concepts and ideas stick, and makes everything stand out. I keep both fine and broad point markers handy here too.

Round Stickers
We will often make decisions using what is called "dot voting." Every member of the team gets so many dots and can vote on actions or items they feel are important. As an example, each member of the Scrum Team gets three dots, and they can place them on whatever items feel most important. They can stack their votes; if something feels extremely important, they can use up to all three dots on one item rather than voting for three different items. If stickers don't work for you, use your markers for the same effect!

Blank printer paper
I often ask my teams to draw. Sometimes I am drawing something and I need them to draw a basic shape with me to continue an activity. Other times I have asked them to take five minutes and sketch something that describes the Sprint. Having blank paper ready if I need it is always important.

Your phone's camera
Take lots of pictures! If the team is playing a game, take pictures while they are doing so! Take one or more pictures of the whiteboard or wall as ideas take shape. Take pictures of the team as they are brainstorming and putting things up on the wall. Pretty much take pictures of everything and then be sure to share them with the team! Sometimes those photos alone will help to reinforce what the team discussed and learned during the Sprint Retrospective.

Other less-used items in my toolkit are:
- 20 feet of light clothesline - because you never know when having everyone hold onto a piece of rope might turn into a good game.

- A deflated beach ball - Only blown up if I need it, but it's too big to leave inflated at my desk!
- Several soft bean bag type balls - because sometimes you need things to toss around the room.
- LEGO® or other building blocks - because building is fun.

After the Retrospective, be sure to take a few minutes and write up a summary of everything that emerged. Transcribe the activity and all notes from the wall, and send it to the team along with all of those photos you took! Make your Retrospective transparent to the team and ONLY to the team.

The most important thing in your toolbox, however, is YOU. Be creative. Practice the art of sketchnotes and use this skill on the whiteboard. Don't be afraid to draw, even if you can't draw a lick. Many times, the roughest of drawings is superior to a work of marker art. Practice drawing stick figures -- you will use them! Be enthusiastic, and your team will catch your enthusiasm, but be ready to put your coaching hat on and contain your enthusiasm if necessary. Be willing to always try something new, to experiment with new formats and techniques. Make your Sprint Retrospectives events that the team looks forward to attending and not just another meeting where we don't accomplish anything.

Keeping Anchors Out of Retrospectives

There are two primary problems I have seen with keeping Retrospectives interesting:

1. Anchoring
2. Repetition

The "classic" Retrospective says we should put three basic questions to our Scrum Teams:
- What went well?
- What didn't go so well?
- What can we do better?

All great questions, and we should be asking them. Kind of. Asking exactly those questions at the end of each iteration, however, becomes stagnant in a hurry. When the team knows exactly what to expect in every Retrospective, it becomes easy to sort of tune out, and you will find the energy being sapped from your Sprint Retrospectives. How then do we inject energy back into the event using everything in our toolkit?

Remind the team of the Retrospective Prime Directive and make sure everyone feels safe sharing their thoughts. I don't do this for every Sprint Retrospective, but from time to time it's good to remind the team that this is their meeting to talk about anything, even when it's hard. Make sure they know that their input is important, and you respect what everyone is saying. Remind them of the Scrum Values, as well, if that is required. The team should be comfortable talking about anything that comes up during the Retrospective.

Going around the room/table/Skype call and asking people to answer each question in turn before moving to the next person leads to the first problem. The first person to chime in provides excellent feedback. After that, it's really easy for everyone to simply say "I agree with..." because the person who has previously spoken provided an anchor. The simplest way to avoid anchoring is to give everyone a chance to provide feedback in a pseudo-bubble. There are a few ways you can do this.

One easy way is to establish the framework for the activity you are doing and explain what you are looking for. For this example, we will use a simple "Start/Stop/Keep" format. Instead of asking one person to provide answers for each before moving on, give a 15-second timebox and have them provide one thing in one category. There is no discussion, just a quick answer. If they can't come up with something, simply say "Pass" and move on to the next person. Go around the room two or three times and record each person's responses on the whiteboard as they come up. After you've gone around and have the most important items to talk about, allow the discussion to take place. Ask should we Start/Stop/Keep things that came up, and see if there are action items that the Scrum Team wants to take on. By limiting the response to only one category, keeping a brisk pace, and holding off all discussion for later, you will start to quickly fill up your whiteboard with great ideas from the team! If you sense that one or more team members are not comfortable sharing their thoughts, that should be a sign that team safety needs to be improved, and maybe a non-verbal way of facilitating the Retrospective is in order.

Another way to get everyone's input is to make maximum use of your sticky notes! If everyone is in the same room (ideally), pass out the sticky notes and pens/markers and give team members the space to write down their thoughts. Then have everyone put their notes up on the whiteboard simultaneously and discuss them all as a team. Use different colored sticky notes for each thing you want to talk about. I would probably use green for "Start," red/pink for "Stop," and blue for "Keep," as an example. Keep in mind how colors denote things to people on the team and use them to your advantage. By adding this extra layer of protection for the team and giving them a couple of minutes in quiet to write their thoughts, you might get answers people wouldn't feel comfortable sharing out loud. More importantly, nobody will know what someone else has written until everyone has posted their sticky notes on the whiteboard. You will find alignment from people on common items, which is an excellent way of quickly determining what is most important to the team and needs more discussion.

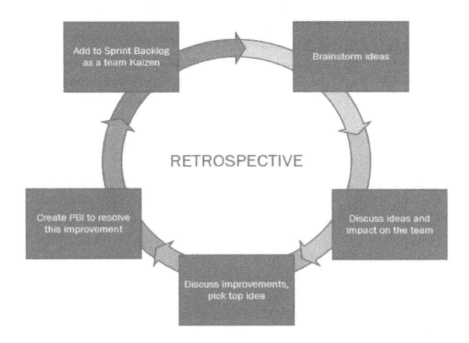

Figure 25 - The Sprint Retrospective Cycle

If the trust isn't quite there on the team yet, have everyone write down answers and pass them to you directly, facedown. You can then transcribe everything onto new sticky notes or write everything on the whiteboard so everything the team sees is in your handwriting and they can't easily identify who wrote what. Be sure to destroy the originals and let the team see you do so if that helps foster a sense of safety. It takes a little longer this way, but if team safety is a problem, this is an excellent way to move forward. Have everyone pass you at least one sticky note of each color, even if that sticky note is blank, so it's impossible for anyone else to tell who did or didn't write what. Establishing this sense of safety will make it easier for the team to openly discuss things later.

Sticky notes are harder to do when using Skype. If you already know what you want to ask the team (and you should!) put those questions into a Google Form and send the link out to everyone the day before the Retrospective. Get everyone to add their thoughts beforehand and bring up the summary to share with everyone who is remote. Use the collected information in exactly the same way you would use a group of sticky notes and let the team discussion happen.

Talk about what people have written down and group items together as themes emerge. See where the team is in agreement and where they see matters differently. Explore those spaces and encourage them to talk to each other and ask questions. Guide the conversation toward coming up with goals for how to move forward without steering the actual discussion. Ask open-ended questions and be prepared for complete silence. Remember that your job is to facilitate, not to supplement the discussion or inject your thoughts unnecessarily. The team may look to you for guidance, or have questions specifically about how they should do something, but this is your opportunity to stay as neutral as possible and coach them along. Encourage them to come up with their own answers as much as possible by asking questions.

Sometimes the team will arrive at a conclusion you have already drawn; more often they will surprise you with insight that you couldn't get on your own. This is ultimately the Scrum Team's meeting, and what they feel is important takes priority. Challenge them to come up with improvements and task them with making those improvements happen.

Repetitive Retrospectives Are Repetitive

I have two approaches to Retrospectives, and I use them both freely. The first is to take the so-called "classic" and find different ways to approach those same questions. Put some kind of fun spin or theme around the entire activity and talk about the good, the bad, and the other. Asking the same "Start/Stop/Keep" questions in every Sprint Retrospective gets boring quickly. Just as anchoring is a problem, running the exact same activity every time will kill your energy. Sometimes I will forgo any questions at all and just start the conversation with a simple "How did this Sprint go?" and let the team take the lead and allow the discussion to take whatever shape they choose. Make the activity fun, get people drawing pictures, and get the team on their feet and moving around. Encourage some kind of kinetic energy in the room rather than just everyone sitting around writing on sticky notes and not talking.

Anything you can do to mix things up, even slightly, and bring a sense of fun is a good thing. Make everyone a superhero and talk about what their powers are and what they are fighting? What's the villain's weakness? What's the scene that plays after the credits roll in their summer blockbuster? The possibilities are really only limited by your imagination.

Sometimes, however, I omit all Inspect and Adapt activities during the Retrospective. Go ahead and yell at me that this isn't Scrum. You're not wrong; the Scrum Guide is pretty clear about that. Sometimes, though, it's important to just change the energy. If the team has been going all out and you can sense that there's some burnout, for example, it's a good time to do something that is just fun and silly, and leave the serious work behind for an hour. Play a game, do some kind of team-building exercise, or just take the team out for ice cream and chat! Break up the pattern, let your team focus on something else for a bit, and watch their energy change.

Another excellent way to change the energy in the room is to have someone else facilitate the Retrospective. I occasionally will ask a fellow Scrum Master to do this for me, and I will take part in the Retrospective along with the rest of the Scrum Team. Sometimes, it's perfectly okay to defer to one of the team members; let them decide what they want to talk about as a team and let the conversation happen. Step in only when needed and let them drive their own Retrospective. Remember that there is often more value in your silence than in your words. Run a Lean Coffee with the team and have a self-determining agenda. Have some games ready for times when you need to mix it up. Bring in a snack for the team (all good meetings have snacks). Go outside on a beautiful day, sit in the sun, and have your Retrospective there. There are infinite possibilities for how you can bring new energy to the event, and I recommend you try them all.

A quick search will point you to several sites that have amazing resources for running fun, non-repetitive Retrospectives. I have used many of them as well as mixed up activities at will, to keep my teams guessing and energized. The goal is always the same; inspecting how the team is working, and coming to some agreement on how we can get better in the next Sprint. The majority of your Retrospectives will accomplish exactly that, no matter how you run them.

I have one activity that I do with each of my teams approximately once per quarter, that I select just because it's fun and gets them talking to each other about something other than work and laughing together. Sometimes at my expense, and that's okay! I absolutely have a rule that I won't ask the team to do something that I wouldn't do myself, and if there's something incredibly silly, I am the first one to do it!

Four Questions - A Team Building exercise

My Four Questions Sprint Retrospective is one that is designed purely for fun and to get the team talking about absolutely anything. This is the activity I repeat from time to time with new questions and different ways to get team members talking to each other. It's an excellent ice breaker for a newly formed team, and a great way to break up the cycle for a mature team and get people just having fun and encouraging team-building.

The basic format is simple, I draw a grid on the whiteboard that looks something like this:

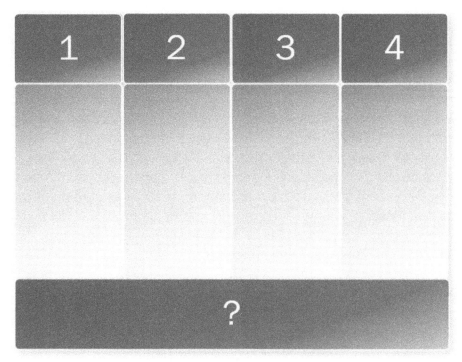

Figure 26 - The Four Questions Grid

I pass out sticky notes to everyone using five different colors -- one per question with a spare thrown in. I ask each question and have everyone write down their answer on the sticky note of the appropriate color. Nothing goes on the whiteboard until we are all done.

The four questions I start with are these:
- What is your fifteen minutes of fame?
- What professional achievement are you most proud of?
- Pirates, Ninjas, or Zombies?
- What is something random about yourself?

I have others, but those four are my traditional go-tos the first time I run this exercise. I do this because it's a mix of business-related info, personal anecdotes, and the just plain silly. As I ask each question, I put a sticky note with that question - using the corresponding color - in the top row of that column. Of course, I also answer the question myself! Once all four questions have been asked, I then call attention to the fifth color and give the team an opportunity to come up with questions of their own. Once we are all done, all of the sticky notes go on the whiteboard in the appropriate column. The team generated questions occupy the entire bottom row.

Now we go around and talk about our answers. I always start, following my rule that I won't ask the team to do something that I won't do. As team members talk about their answer, allow others to ask questions if they are curious. Once all questions have been answered, go through the ones the team generated and answer those too! Let the person who wrote the question go first.

Other excellent questions I have used are:
- What is your favorite movie?
- What person do you admire most?
- What is your favorite place you have traveled to?
- What was the last TV show you binge-watched?
- What was the last book you read for pleasure?
- Black licorice, yes or no?
- What is something you did as a teen that your mom doesn't know about?
- What hobbies do you have to unwind after work?

The possibilities are absolutely endless and only limited by your ability to be creative. Let the team have fun, laugh, and learn about each other. It's a great way to break things up!

Scrum Radar - How focused on the Values are we?

It's important to me that my Scrum Teams keep the Scrum Values in mind, and how better to do this than during a Retrospective? I recently noticed that there were some problems facing one of my teams and wanted to find a way to foster an open discussion and see where the Team would go with it. It took some brainstorming, and then the perfect approach hit me. This is a perfect team radar exercise.

Draw your Radar

If you haven't done any team radar before, this is a very powerful tool to get an idea for how your teams are feeling and generate some possibilities for how to improve. The general idea is as follows:

1. On your whiteboard/easel/wall - draw a 5-line starfish diagram.
2. Each arm of the starfish should be labeled with one of the Scrum Values:
   a. Courage
   b. Commitment
   c. Focus
   d. Openness
   e. Respect
3. Each arm has a scale starting at 0 in the center to 10 at the tip of the arm.
4. A sheet of paper is handed to each member of the Team. You can have a copy of the starfish on the paper or you can ask them to draw a copy on their sheet. I generally like to have the team members draw as it adds a little reinforcement to what we are doing.
5. Review the Scrum Values with the team! Let them ask questions if they aren't clear on any of them!

   These next steps are done in silence. Allow each team member the safety to reflect his/her own thoughts without any discussion. Once the team radar is complete, we can discuss our findings, but for now working quietly wins.

6. Each member now scores how they think the team does at living each of the Scrum Values - 0 being we don't do this at all, 10 being we personify this - and make a dot on the corresponding arm of the starfish on their paper.
7. Once the dots are drawn, each member should connect the dots on their paper, drawing a pentagon of sorts.
8. Each member is given a different colored marker, and asked to recreate their drawing on the wall/whiteboard/easel.

The completed radar will look something like this:

125

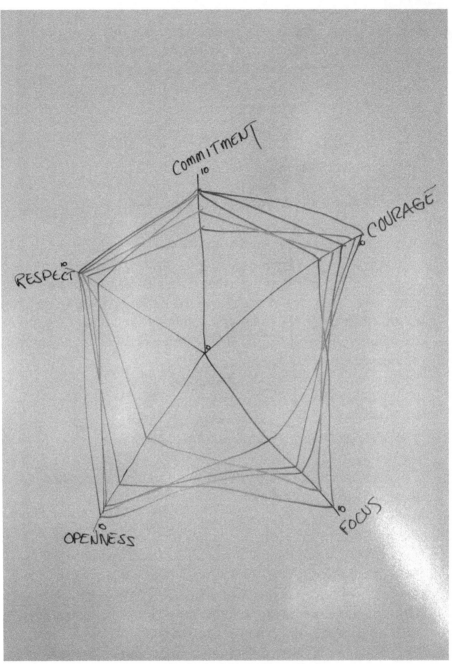

Figure 27 - Sprint Values Team Radar

When everyone is done, allow the team a minute to look at the results and think about it.

- Where are we in agreement?
- Where do we have a strong disconnect?
- How can we push the lower values up, and how can we bring widely distributed answers closer together?

As you can see in this sample, the team here feels there is great Respect on the team, which is fantastic! They feel pretty strongly about Commitment and Courage, and there's not much disagreement there. Focus and Openness are potential weak spots here, and these are absolutely items to discuss.

Collect Thoughts

Ask questions and facilitate the conversation without guiding the team toward any answers you may have in mind. Let them talk and see what they can come up with! When I ran this recently, I was pleased to see that without any prompting by me the team found the same weak spots that I had noticed before running the exercise, and they were able to come up with some ideas about how to adapt and make improvements. If there's more than one potential trouble spot, it might be easier to let the team pick one area to focus on in the discussion and come up with ideas for how to make it better. Don't try to solve everything in one meeting.

You will note that I don't put any indicators to mark where the values between 0 and 10 fall on the arms of the starfish. I like to leave it a little vague and allow the members of the team to interpret where they think things fall, as it opens up the drawing a little more and provides opportunity for discussion. That discussion might be that everyone is actually in agreement on how we are doing, and that's great! If it's easier for your team to mark the plot points on each arm (and they don't have to be perfect), go for it!

The radar itself is only a tool, the important thing – as in many retrospectives – is the discussion that follows. Getting your team to actively think about the Scrum Values helps to reinforce them and their importance. If you notice numbers on the low side, or arms with a disparity of values, it's important to repeat this exercise in a future Retrospective to bring the pillars of Transparency, Inspection, and Adaptation to bear on how we are doing as a group.

Team radar is a powerful tool in your Retrospective toolkit and you should use it wisely. You are certainly not limited to only the Scrum Values on the five arms of the starfish (nor are you limited to exactly five arms). You can and should use a team radar for anything that you want to try to quantify and measure as a team, and you can gauge progress toward any goals by running the exercise as needed.

Kaizen Master

Kaizen (n): a Japanese business philosophy of continuous improvement of working practices, personal efficiency, etc.
I have used the words "inspect" and "adapt" frequently in this book. The word "Kaizen" simplifies this philosophy of constant inspection and adaptation, combined with complete transparency, into a single word. This is our entire empirical process summarized. The more mature our Scrum Teams are, the more important our Kaizen becomes. We want to always find ways in which we can get better, and have a mindset that fosters that growth.

The outcome of (nearly) every Sprint Retrospective is one or more Kaizen. The team should be taking everything in the Retrospective and using it to determine what to do next. New teams will have simple Kaizen, and mature teams will have ideas that push their boundaries and force them to look hard at how they are working. The Kaizen the team accepts becomes both an action item and a goal for the new Sprint, and it lives on the Sprint Backlog for all to see. It's important that we make these ideas visible, not just to the team, but to anyone who is interested, so we can see how we did.

The SMART rules we apply to any goal should apply to the Kaizen we choose. It's important that we only take on those actions and improvements we can achieve in the new Sprint, and only those items the Scrum Team is able to achieve themselves. We cannot make sweeping organizational changes at the team level, we cannot change the seating chart in our office or implement mandatory half-hour nap periods after lunch and a company-supplied massage studio for stress relief, no matter how much we might want such things. As a team, we can only impact how we work amongst ourselves, and how we interact with other teams. We can't change how everyone else works, and we should not commit to a Kaizen that requires someone else to take action.

Taking on an improvement is not something the team does lightly. Much thought and discussion should happen regarding every possible idea they have as to how to get better until they settle on the one or two most important things to get done immediately in the new Sprint. I have seen instances where teams try to take on five or six Kaizen, only to get none of them done because they overcommitted themselves. It is always better to take on one thing that the team has absolute confidence in their ability to complete. Making even one improvement per Sprint will yield huge differences over time. Don't try to change the entire world at once.

As Scrum Master or Product Owner, it's okay to ask the team how YOU are doing and take on a personal Kaizen also! You are there to support the team, and if there is something you can do better, that's an excellent thing to commit to. Be unafraid of asking for feedback and make sure you do what you commit to. Your example will guide the team and make them less fearful of making changes themselves.

The important thing about Kaizen is that's it's a mindset. We take on specific tasks with a goal toward always making improvements to how we work. Like Scrum itself, it's easy to just do the things without understanding why. It's only when we change how we think about improving our teams that true change happens. Foster a Kaizen mindset and philosophy with your teams and watch as the barriers come down and explosive growth begins.

VIII - Building a Better...

Scrum Master

For starters, let's look to the Scrum Guide to see what it has to say about the role of the Scrum Master[xv]:

The Scrum Master
The Scrum Master is accountable for establishing Scrum as defined in the Scrum Guide. They do this by helping everyone understand Scrum theory and practice, both within the Scrum Team and the organization.

The Scrum Master is accountable for the Scrum Team's effectiveness. They do this by enabling the Scrum Team to improve its practices, within the Scrum framework.

Scrum Masters are true leaders who serve the Scrum Team and the larger organization.

The Scrum Master serves the Scrum Team in several ways, including:

- Coaching the team members in self-management and cross-functionality;
- Helping the Scrum Team focus on creating high-value Increments that meet the Definition of Done;
- Causing the removal of impediments to the Scrum Team's progress; and,
- Ensuring that all Scrum events take place and are positive, productive, and kept within the timebox.

The Scrum Master serves the Product Owner in several ways, including:

- Helping find techniques for effective Product Goal definition and Product Backlog management;
- Helping the Scrum Team understand the need for clear and concise Product Backlog items;
- Helping establish empirical product planning for a complex environment; and,
- Facilitating stakeholder collaboration as requested or needed.

The Scrum Master serves the organization in several ways, including:

- Leading, training, and coaching the organization in its Scrum adoption;
- Planning and advising Scrum implementations within the organization;
- Helping employees and stakeholders understand and enact an empirical approach for complex work; and,
- Removing barriers between stakeholders and Scrum Teams.

Okay, there's a lot there to digest, so let's pick it apart section by section, and see what we can get from each one. For now, let's sort of take the high-level view of what it says about this thing we do. The opening sentences gives us a great place to start:

"The Scrum Master is accountable for establishing Scrum as defined in the Scrum Guide. They do this by helping everyone understand Scrum theory and practice, both within the Scrum Team and the organization.

The Scrum Master is accountable for the Scrum Team's effectiveness. They do this by enabling the Scrum Team to improve its practices, within the Scrum framework.

Scrum Masters are true leaders who serve the Scrum Team and the larger organization."

There's a lot there for only five sentences. Let's start with the underlying fact that YOU need to understand Scrum inside and out. Read the Scrum Guide. Read it again. It's not long, but it has everything you need to be successful. Your responsibility to the Scrum Team is to help them to fully understand and embrace Scrum, and to feel empowered every step of the way. You don't need to transform everything at once. Find the spots where you can help the team to make incremental improvements and act on those spots! The phrase "Inspect and Adapt" gets used a lot in Scrum, and with good reason. During early stages of Scrum, you will be the one doing a lot of the I&A work and subtly guiding the team along the way.

You'll notice the phrase "servant-leader" isn't there anymore. You are there to lead the team on the Scrum path, but you don't do so by telling them what to do. You are there to coach, to listen, and to assist. You are there to help the team learn and improve. But it's never about you, and you actually hold no real authority over the team, as they do not report to you. The two strongest tools you have are your ears. By listening to the team and helping them to become amazing, you lead both the team and yourself to greater heights.

You are also a protector for the Developers, helping to shield them from distraction so they can focus on the commitments they have made. You have to help people understand what the team's focus is, while also listening to what they need and helping to triage the situation. Sometimes it's important that the team hear something immediately, other times you may need to direct them to the Product Owner because they're looking for something to go on the Backlog.

As the Scrum Master, you are the rock of the team in many ways. You are the person the team will look to for guidance when they aren't sure about something. You are the person the Product Owner will rely on to help the team deliver the maximum value to your stakeholders. You are the person the organization will expect to create positive change. Conduct your own personal retrospective and look for ways to push yourself beyond your comfort zone!

Scrum Master Service to the Product Owner

The Scrum Master and the Product Owner have a special working relationship. The two roles could not be more different, and having a strong working arrangement between the two is crucial for the Scrum Team to thrive. The Scrum Master works very closely with the Product Owner on many of her tasks to make sure she is effectively working with the Developers.

The Scrum Master helps the Product Owner manage the Product Backlog. He understands that the PO always needs to be looking forward and keep enough in the Product Backlog for the next few Sprints. He facilitates refinement activities and Sprint Planning, making sure there is alignment between the PO and the Developers. He coaches the Scrum Team on what constitutes a good Product Backlog Item and how to write excellent acceptance criteria. He is there to assist the Product Owner with release planning if she needs assistance. A great Scrum Master lives in the Product Backlog nearly as much as his Product Owner. He is watching for warning signs that the Backlog is in trouble and actively taking steps to correct potential issues.

James of Team PAWS understands this. He checks the Product Backlog on a regular basis to make sure it is always healthy. He looks to see that Backlog Items are clearly defined and make sense to anyone who is reading them, not just Sarah or the Developers. The Backlog should have some sense of cohesion that aligns with the product vision as he understands it, and he can see the strategy looking forward. He is looking to make sure that Backlog Items are not overly technical in nature, as technical details should be emerging as the team refines and plans those items. James is also always cognizant of having lots of Spikes throughout the backlog, as this is a sign that the team is unsure of what they need to be doing and some additional attention needs to be paid to what is going on.

Some important notes:

It is absolutely possible for the Scrum Master to also be a one of the Developers. This is actually not an uncommon occurrence. It is imperative that the Product Owner and Scrum Master roles are not filled by the same person. The responsibilities of these roles are in conflict with each other, and it is impossible to achieve the full potential of Scrum when sharing these roles. The Product Owner naturally wants to always push the Developers to deliver more and more value in every Sprint, potentially to a point where it is not realistic. The Scrum Master is there to protect the team from themselves, and possibly even from the Product Owner in this case. He knows the team's limit based on their historical velocity and will not let the team take on more work than they can handle.

The Product Owner has absolute authority over her Backlog. Help her realize that she owns the Product Backlog and is a subject matter expert on her product. James knows that Sarah is awesome at what she does and does everything he can to assist her. He clearly communicates to everyone that they don't have to always agree with every decision Sarah makes, but they must always respect her decisions. This is not just limited to the Developers, but to the entire organization. He helps to empower the PO to be highly effective at her job.

Scrum Master Service to the Scrum Team

When it comes to the Scrum Team as a whole, the Scrum Master is there to lead through service. He assists them with being truly self-organizing and self-managing. During Sprint Planning, he is there to help the team create their Sprint Backlog, and protects them from carrying too much work and overcommitting. The Scrum Master helps the team to be cross-functional, encouraging them to help each other out on all tasks, and facilitating the arts of pair-programming and swarming.

He wants the team to deliver high-quality high-value product. The Scrum Master recognizes that driving value is how the team is ultimately measured, and that their success is his success. He actively removes impediments raised by the team and coaches them on ways to remove ones that don't need his direct intervention. It's worth noting here that close to 100% of impediments come down to poor communication. We find ourselves with a dependency that becomes an impediment to our progress because we aren't getting a response from another team. Sometimes, just having a Developer copy you on a follow-up email is enough to elicit a response! If not, go get the answer for your team, so the Developers can focus on creating value.

As with the Product Owner, he knows that face-to-face communication is the best way to interact with the team. The Scrum Master lives the Scrum Values and leads by example, showing Commitment, Courage, Focus, Openness, and Respect at all times. While the team never actually reports to the Scrum Master, they know that he is always trying to lead them in the right direction and get them to be their absolute best. He has a plethora of coaching techniques available to him and is both willing and able to coach the team -- as a whole or as individuals -- on any matter that he sees the need for. In the case of a new Scrum Team, the Scrum Master serves as a teacher, coach, and mentor to the entire team.

Scrum Master Service to the Organization

The Scrum Master's service to the organization is wholly different than his service to his Product Owner or his Developers. A good Scrum Master has the ability to change his team, but a great Scrum Master has the ability to change his organization. He leads and coaches the organization if they are new to Scrum and spearheads efforts to stand up new Scrum Teams in a mature organization. The organization recognizes that he is an expert in his field and respects his opinion and his knowledge, which he shares eagerly.

He works with employees and stakeholders to understand why Scrum works and how an Agile organization will benefit all involved. He gets excited when a new Scrum Team forms -- even if he is not working with that team -- because he knows how it will change the organization. The Scrum Master knows in his heart that Scrum works best when the entire organization changes to become more Agile, and he is capable of leading the charge in that effort.

Great Scrum Masters are always collaborating. They love to share ideas, get new insights, and help each other out. They are willing to facilitate events for each other in order to drive their teams ahead and change the dynamic. They are always brainstorming new ways to facilitate change. Putting the entire organization on their collective backs and carrying them across the Scrum finish line is not something that the Scrum Masters shy away from, but a task they take on happily.

It's not about YOU

Sometimes the biggest challenge of being an effective Scrum Master is learning to put yourself aside. We are there to serve the team and lead through our service to them. Servant-leader is a challenging mantle to wear but wear it we must. You aren't in charge of things, you don't tell the team what to do, and when someone does something in a way you wouldn't, it's not the time to stand up and yell. Are you calling attention to yourself? Or guiding your Team toward success? If there's even a little danger of the former, it's time to step back, use silence to your advantage, and then see how you can best serve your team while coaching them on how to make improvements.

We all want to succeed personally. As intrinsically motivated professionals, we strive to get better at what we do. The goals of mastery, autonomy, and purpose guide us forward to become the best version of ourselves at work. As a Scrum Master, this means taking focus away from what you are doing and putting it purely on your team. When our teams are successful, so are we. It's all about doing everything humanly possible to help them become even more amazing.

Scrum Master is one of the few jobs where you are actively working to make yourself redundant. We want to get our teams to a point where we are no longer needed, but still wanted because of the value we provide to the team. The best feedback from any Scrum Team is when you are moving on and they resist because you are such an integral part of the team. It's good when you know that if you miss one of the events, the team will get it all done in your absence. Your success is purely dependent on your ability to put yourself aside and become obsessed with driving your team ahead. Remove impediments as though your life depended on it. If there are organizational barriers to getting your teams to a point where they are intrinsically motivated, actively try to change the culture to remove those barriers. Know that you aren't going to get the glory, but you are there to help your team do so. Your glory comes when the team learns something, fearlessly tries something new, and delivers critical value to the stakeholders in a timely manner. When you see your team members swarming on work, communicating and collaborating effortlessly, and they have increased their velocity along the way, you are doing an amazing job. If you find yourself actively questioning if you are doing the right thing, you probably are. A great Scrum Master is always challenging himself to do better and is relentlessly looking for ways to improve.

As a Scrum Master, your toolset is almost entirely revolving around soft skills. Your people skills and ability to be an effective coach and communicator are the most important things you have. If you have a technical background, it's easy to put yourself in the shoes of the Developers and come up with an idea of how you would engineer a solution. It's critical that you don't do so. It's easy to disagree with the Product Owner when she wants to push the team harder to deliver more value. It's important that you do so with empirical data on your side, and in a way that leaves your PO feeling like you have the same goal but know what the team's limits are. When your Product Owner has mastered writing effective Product Backlog Items, and is making excellent use of Backlog Refinement and using important techniques like Story Mapping, you have done your job to perfection.

It's important that the entire Scrum Team knows you are an important member, and that having you there makes it easier for them to focus on their jobs, because you always have the team's back. One of my former Scrum Teams said that I - as their Scrum Master - was the guy sitting in a bunker armed with an automatic weapon, keeping intruders at bay. Having that protection made it feel safe for them to block out distractions and collaborate on the important work they were doing. Yours is the voice that says "It is okay to try something and fail, because in failure lies growth." Being able to put yourself and your wants aside to focus purely on the team can be frustrating. Part of being a great Scrum Master is the ability to master yourself and know when to step back.

It's good to be passionate, and it's great that you want to help the team by assuming some of the load. The trick lies in finding that magical middle ground where the team can thrive without you being involved in everything they do. Watch for the warning signs and be ready to take a step back when you notice them, and then watch your team grow!

Product Owner

As Product Owner, one is focused on exactly one thing; value. The Product Owner's job description could easily read "Maximizes the Value in her Product." How she determines value is completely up to her, of course, and will vary from product to product. It might even change from one day to the next as she gains new insight. Ultimately, she is the single source of truth on where value lies and how to determine it, and her decision is final. Others in the organization can certainly make an argument to persuade her to value something more highly, but they cannot change the Product Backlog. She is the ultimate arbiter of what goes into the Product Backlog and how it is ordered. Where her product is concerned, she is effectively a mini-CEO and her decisions are final.

The Product Backlog should be well refined at all times, reflecting work to be done in the next several Sprints, as part of a larger Roadmap. The Product Owner knows that Roadmap and has a clear vision for the Product that can be executed by the Developers. She spends time with stakeholders to get their feedback and understand their wants and needs. She invites appropriate stakeholders to the Sprint Review so they can see a new working increment of software and provide feedback in real time. Their feedback helps to update the Product Backlog and can help inform your decision of whether an increment is ready for release. The Product Owner understands that getting this vital feedback drives more value into the product, with the ultimate measure being market reception. It is only through releasing an increment into the market that value can be fully measured. She knows that revenue alone doesn't measure value, but that there are many factors that go into its assessment. How she measures value prior to release is up to her, and she alone is responsible for ordering items in the Product Backlog. She knows her customers and works to exceed their expectations.

The Product Owner collaborates closely with the Developers daily. This close working relationship helps the entire Scrum Team make critical decisions about both effort and value; keeping those two important factors in balance. She prefers face-to-face communication with the Scrum Team over all else, recognizing that conversation is always better than an email or phone call. This collaboration helps ensure that the increment being created is adding value that aligns with the needs of stakeholders and users. A great Product Owner also understands the impact of Technical Debt on the team. Technical Debt almost always means that a greater percentage of a product's budget will be spent in maintenance, as defects are found in production, or as code needs to be refactored (or worse - rewritten) to pay off that debt. This will, in turn, mean that a smaller amount of the Developers' capacity will be spend on creating new value, and will slow down the overall velocity and time to get new features released. Value and functionality are where the Product Owner spends her time focusing. The estimates of the team and their velocity are only important to her so that she can predict when value might be delivered.

One key point: the Product Owner is one person. It's possible, even likely, that a PO will have more than one product she is responsible for, but there can never be more than one PO on a single product. There might be Business Analysts or other proxies working with the Product Owner, but the PO is ultimately responsible for every aspect of the product and the value being created. She knows how to work at the strategic, tactical, and operational levels, and is an effective communicator with everyone.

The Sprint Review and Backlog Refinement are truly owned by the Product Owner, working with the Scrum Master to facilitate as needed. The Sprint Review is NOT a demo of code from the Developers to the Product Owner, but a chance to go over the entire Done increment with stakeholders, review progress, and adjust plans for future Sprints. Changes that are suggested from the Sprint Review can go into the Product Backlog and be further refined by the PO and the Developers before going into the Sprint Backlog. The Product Owner also plays a crucial role in setting the Sprint Goal. It might be that she has a goal in mind going into Sprint Planning, and asks the team to select Backlog

Items to fit with that Goal. She attends every Sprint Retrospective, because her input is valuable to the entire team. She tries to attend the Daily Scrum Meeting when she can, but understands that it is the Developers' meeting and she is there only to answer questions or participate in 16th minute discussions.

The Product Owner helps to shape the team's Definition of Done. She recognizes that having this clearly spelled out for the entire Scrum team increases transparency into the state of the work. She has faith that at the end of every Sprint the Developers have provided a usable increment that she can potentially release to the market.

Developers

As we have seen, the Developers own how value is created for the product. They have absolute control over architecture, design, and all technical decisions about how the product is built and implemented. The team is completely empowered with how they work and what they work on. They own the Sprint Backlog fully, and nobody can make a change to the Sprint Backlog without the Developers' blessing.

A great team understands that "Done" is their responsibility, and they will pull out all stops to get there within the Sprint's timebox. Because they have a "T-shaped" skill set, all members of the team are able to work on whatever is needed at any time. They recognize that no individual members of the team own the work, but the entire team shares responsibility equally for their success and failure. Work is not assigned to members of the team -- they talk to each other and come up with the best plan of how to attack any problem they face. They are both self-organizing and self-managing. Nobody needs to oversee all aspects of their work 24/7, just as nobody needs to assign work to them. They alone, as a group, decide what they are going to do and how they are going to do it with no outside interference. Great Developers are focused on doing exactly one thing at a time and doing it well. They understand that context switching leads to wasted time and effort, and they look to minimize that waste.

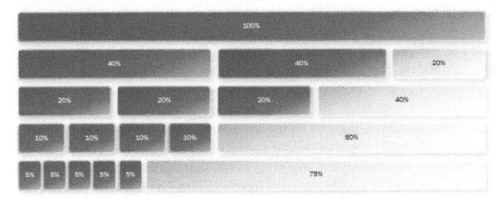

Figure 28 - The Effect of Context Switching (Weinberg 1992).[xvi]

The Developers live the Scrum Values. They understand that all of these are important to their ability to work together every day and produce high-quality high-value product. They know that continued technical excellence is vital to their success. They do not take on Technical Debt lightly, and when they do incur it, they clearly communicate to the Product Owner so that she fully understands the impact of such a decision. They are always willing to experiment and unafraid of failure. They are more afraid of staying in the same place than they are to fail and learn from that experience. They are always striving to make their code better, applying the Boy Scout rule and leaving things a little cleaner than when they got there. They refactor mercilessly.

The Developers are comfortable with Test Driven Development (TDD) and pair programming. They understand that constant peer review and an unflinching commitment to quality is the best way to drive their product forward quickly and efficiently. They don't see pair programming as wasting one developer's time, as it is truly not idle time but time spend in constant review of code to make the best possible decisions. They recognize that the entire team is smarter than the smartest member of the team and strive to make all important decisions as a whole. The team is excellent at Product Backlog Refinement and excels at breaking down stories to individual tasks. They recognize that the fastest way to complete work in the Sprint Backlog is to swarm on it, dividing the tasks among developers and making sure they integrate their work frequently.

142

The Developers own their Sprint Backlog. Once they have committed to their forecast, nobody can move work in or out of the Sprint Backlog without the team's blessing. They update the board themselves, not relying on the Scrum Master or others to do it for them. They recognize that the entire organization is looking at the board for a real-time picture of how their Sprint is progressing. They also realize that they can't be going all out all the time and build in some slack time for things they can't foresee.

The relationship between the Developers, the Product Owner, and the Scrum Master is important to the team's success. It is only when all three roles are actively doing their part that the team can truly succeed. The Developers rely on the Product Owner to provide an ordered, well-refined Product Backlog, to provide insights into what customers -- internal and external -- are looking for, and clarity into what the completed increment should look like. They rely on the Scrum Master to help facilitate events, to actively remove -- or provide assistance in removing -- impediments, and to keep them honest with each other about how they are working. They trust each other and the other roles completely. They communicate constantly, whether face-to-face or via whichever digital tool they are using. Great Developers recognize that the days of each team member putting on headphones and going completely heads down are in the past, and it is only through constant collaboration that they can truly be amazing.

Perhaps most importantly, the Developers trust each other and knows how to have fun together. They take their work seriously, but that doesn't mean they don't find time to laugh or to celebrate their successes. They know that going out for a team lunch or a team happy hour can sometimes do more for team building than anything they do at the office. They enjoy working together and feel like there is no task they cannot accomplish.

IX – Coaching and Collaboration

First, Let's All Agree on Some Things

Working Agreements are important. One of the earliest things we can do to come together as a Scrum Team is to discuss what our working agreements are as a team. This is our contract with ourselves concerning how we are going to work – and succeed – together. It's not vital that every team establish working agreements, but I certainly recommend it. For new teams in particular, it helps to get everyone on the same page. Esther Derby wrote at length about the importance of Working Agreements, and she's exactly right.[xvii]

If the idea of a working agreement sounds daunting, you're already overthinking it. In its most basic form, the working agreement is simply a series of statements that the team has agreed is important with regards to their values and how they work together as a whole. Forming one couldn't be simpler. I will often do this in the very first Sprint Retrospective I have with a team. If it's an existing team, it helps me to understand what the team's norms are, and if it's a brand-new team, it becomes an instant team building exercise.

You only need a couple of things to get started and create a working agreement:
- Sticky Notes
- Pens
- The Scrum Team

Okay, you will need something else too, but that's all you need to get started.

- Pass out sticky notes to everyone (and have a couple of spare pens for those people who invariably forget to bring one).
- Have everyone brainstorm about things that are important to them and write those ideas on sticky notes. One item per sticky note! Ideally, everyone comes up with 2-3 solid ideas.

145

- Timebox this to no more than five minutes. I've had luck with three minutes, but you know your team better than I do.
- All ideas go up on the wall. We don't care about duplicates yet.
- Have each person review what he/she wrote with the team and why it's important. Start grouping together duplicates on the wall as they emerge at this point.
- Once everyone has had a chance to review their ideas with the team, use dot voting to come up with what the team feels are the most important items. Give everyone at least three votes.
- Pick the top items the team voted on. This is your working agreement.

Now take those items and write them out nice and big somewhere in the team room! I prefer to use a sticky note easel pad, write them all out, and put the sheet up where everyone can see it during the day. Using an easel pad also lets me move the sheet with our working agreement into a separate meeting room if needed, to keep everyone mindful of what our team expects of ourselves.

Some sample items I have seen in working agreements:
- We will only have one conversation at a time and will listen to what is being said without interrupting the speaker.
- We will only commit to items that meet our Definition of Ready.
- We will not mark any work as done that does not meet our DoD.
- We will be on time for the Daily Scrum Meeting and will adhere to the 15-minute timebox.

Your teams will come up with their own items, values, and group norms that they feel are important. Don't guide them down a particular path, but listen to the team and facilitate discussion. Your teams might surprise you with what they come up with. It's important to revisit the working agreement from time to time. There may be things on the agreement that the team feels are no longer important to emphasize, or new things they would like to have agreed upon as a team. This is very much a living document that should mature with the team and reflect who they are.

Exposing Our Faults and Learning to Embrace the Pain

Scrum does not solve your problems, it exposes them.

That simple statement is incredibly profound, and it struck me immediately. Read it again and let it sink in.

That simple sentence cuts right to the heart of things. Too many times I have heard from teams that they wish they had a finalized design before they start coding, or they had created a fully defined architecture and detailed plan for the next several weeks. I have seen crestfallen looks, heard audible sighs, and witnessed eyes rolling when I have to gently break it to them that these things just won't be happening.

That's not how any of this works.

Scrum works not because it's a magic bullet that will suddenly make everything in your development shop perfect. It works because it shines a light on where the problems are and empowers you to make the corrections that you need. As a Scrum Team, it gives us, opportunities to continuously inspect our progress and make adjustments. It encourages all of us to try things and gives us space to fail. In fact, a certain amount of failure is a good thing. When we look at all of the Scrum ceremonies (Daily Scrum, Sprint Planning, Sprint Review, Sprint Retrospective), we see a chance in every single one to make changes based on the empirical evidence of how the team is performing and the challenges they are facing.

That doesn't mean it's easy.

We aren't comfortable seeing our problems and facing them. Our instinct is one of preservation, and you'll see team members get defensive when the weak spots are made visible. I've seen all of these things happen:
- Members offer excuses for why something went wrong, rather than working to solve it.
- People wish we could "do things the old way."

- Team members get angry, or worse, throw another member of their team under the bus to protect themselves, because they feel like there is a risk in being anything less than perfect.
- A Scrum Master's coaching skills tested to their utmost.

I can say from experience that there have been moments when I've been tempted to just walk away from the hard work because I feared confrontation, or had reached the end of my rope with someone who just didn't seem to get it. Scrum exposed MY problem, and I was able to step back, reflect on what was actually happening, ask myself the five whys, and come up with a way to work through the issue and get everything back on track. I can honestly say that I am a better Scrum Master because of it.

This was HARD.

Seeing team members going through the same thing - team members you work with every day and have a professional relationship (if not a true friendship) with - is no easier. Because we care about our teams, we want to protect them from all of these issues. In truth, we aren't doing them any service by shielding them from themselves! Yours is the voice of reassurance.

Fortunately, we have plenty of tools at our fingertips to help us with all of these things...

Shhhhh - The Strength of Silence

Picture this: Your team (or someone on the team) comes to you looking for help. They ask you a question. What do you do?

You answer it, right? That's the normal response. By nature, we want to help others (well, most of us do), and that means answering their questions, and sometimes even rolling up our sleeves and helping with the actual work.

How about this situation: You're facilitating a Sprint Retrospective for your Scrum Team and you ask them a question. Nobody answers. Maybe your question was too hard, or they aren't comfortable providing the answer, so you wait a short amount of time and start talking again -- either giving them the answer, or leading them toward the one you have in mind.

What if I were to tell you that might be the wrong thing to do?

As a Scrum Master, one of the most potent tools you have is silence. Keeping your mouth closed is easy, but it's also one of the hardest things to practice and teach yourself. I know that for me I had to fight every instinct I had to learn this one. Being quiet takes work!

But here's the thing: When you become comfortable with your own silence, you allow your teams to grow. When a question is asked -- whether in a team discussion or in a one-on-one setting -- don't answer right away. However long you think is a good pause before you answer, wait three to four times that long. Let the silence get uncomfortable and read the energy of the room.

Don't focus on the fact that you aren't talking, focus on how people are reacting. Read their body language and listen to what they are not telling you. You will naturally start to come up what your answer might be; resist the urge to do so! Keep yourself actively listening through the silence.

When you do this, one of two things will happen:
1. You give yourself extra time to compose your response and make sure you are giving the right answer (or asking a better question), should you choose to do so.

   More often, however...

2. The person will provide their own answer, or someone else on the team will, allowing you to stay in active listening mode and feel where your input is actually needed!

People don't like silence. Most people will instinctively try to fill the silence by speaking up rather than letting that awkward uncomfortable silence linger. More often than not, they will answer their own questions, or at least come up with a more insightful question than the one that was originally asked.

Your knowledge and insight are important to the team. Your silence can be even more important, because in that silence they have the opportunity to stretch out beyond their comfort zone and to grow. The trick lies in knowing how long to let that silence hang, and when they really do need some of your sage-like wisdom. Growth happens in those uncomfortable moments.

Dancing out of the Coaching Death Spiral

First things first. This entire section was inspired by an amazing post by Stephanie Ockerman[xviii]. If you don't already read her blog, you need to fix that right now. She offers amazing insights and is an incredible voice for Scrum.

If you just put this down to go read everything in her blog, I don't take offense.

She describes a pattern early in her post that really got me to thinking about my own coaching style and where things can go wrong. I call this the Coaching Death Spiral, but feel free to come up with whatever better name suits your purpose.

In short, here's the Death Spiral pattern:
- We doubt ourselves -- not sure if we are asking the right questions and saying the right things.
- Once that doubt sets in, we overthink everything.
- We become so involved in our own heads that we aren't actively listening anymore.
- We start missing important cues in tone, body language, or even in the actual words someone is saying.

- Effective coaching has stopped; we've lost the person we are supposed to be coaching.

You can see how each step in the spiral feeds off the one before it, and that once you start down this path, it can become very difficult to escape. I've done this, and I'm quite confident in saying that I will likely do it again, even knowing what's happening. We're human and these things happen.

What's really important is to recognize what can happen and think about how we avoid it in the first place.

It all starts with that first line. We won't always ask the right questions or have the exact perfect thing to say at any given moment. Every single coaching conversation is different -- even when you're coaching the same person on something you've coached them on previously:
- The context for that conversation has changed.
- It's a different time of the day.
- One (or both) of you didn't get a good night's sleep, or hasn't had enough coffee yet.
- Your horoscope told you it's going to be a bad day.

Whatever the circumstances might be, there is always something different and unique about every single coaching event. Going into coaching with any kind of pre-scripted agenda simply isn't going to work, because you don't have all of the information you need until you're well into the event. It's okay to have some thoughts in mind, but those might not actually be what the person you're talking to needs in that moment, and sticking to your talking points could lose the person just as quickly as getting sucked into the Death Spiral.

It's chaos, I know.

To quote directly from Stephanie's amazing post: "We must be willing to dance in this moment."

I LOVE this; that line inspired me.

You are going into a coaching event with someone – whether one on one, or in a group setting – and you don't know what's about to happen:

- When the conversation starts, the music has begun.
- Take your partner and start to dance.
  (Not literally. It might be weird. Unless you actually work in a dance studio.)
- You don't know what the band or DJ is going to play next, just as you don't know where the conversation is going to go.
- You know you want to keep dancing with this person, so you adjust. You find a rhythm and go with it.
- During any given dance, you don't know exactly what you're going to do, you just know you're going to move together and share that moment.
- You will take cues from your dance partner. Sometimes you will lead, sometimes they will lead, and it will all work out great.
- Those cues might be verbal; they might be from making eye contact; they might be in how they are actually moving. All of these things are important.
- The dance can create an emotional connection. Don't shy away from this!
- You may be tired when you finally stop, but it was worth every minute.

Be in the moment. Enjoy the dance and pay attention to what your dance partner is doing. Listen to everything they say, and more to the things they don't. All of these things will give you important clues about what that person wants or needs from this time.

Be there with them. Take your cues from everything the person you are coaching is telling you. You don't have to get it perfect every time, but you do need to be in the moment with them and willing to take them out onto the dance floor and spin around a few times.

Scrum Parenting (and How to Avoid It)

Let's borrow an analogy or two from youth athletics, shall we?

You know them. You might even have been one of them at some point. (Or you are one right now!) The mom who over-nurtures her team, taking on every possible task because nobody else can do it as well. The dad who makes a spectacle of himself from the stands, screaming at the kids, the coach, the officials, and the other parents. Go ahead and reverse the genders on those examples, I've certainly seen it work both ways! If you're nodding your head right about now, you can probably already guess where I'm going with this.

As a Scrum Master, it's incredibly easy to fall into the trap of parenting your team. I'd even say it's one of the first traps we need to overcome on our journey from being a novice Scrum Master to being something better. Learning how to recognize the signs of Scrum Parenting, and how to avoid the perils therein, is essential.

Impediments
The Scrum Guide states that one of the key roles of the Scrum Master is "removing impediments to the Developers' progress." This is absolutely true. The Scrum Parent takes it personally, making it his or her mission to do absolutely everything to clear the path for the team. But sometimes the best way to remove an impediment is to ask the team how to remove it and let them solve their own problem. Empower your team to handle impediments that don't need to be escalated to you. Often, they don't need you to do the actual work, but just to coach them through the problem. Allow the team to learn.

Access to the Team
This goes with the first point, really. It is important to shield the Developers from things -- sometimes. The key here is sometimes. When it comes to feedback from the Product Owner and Stakeholders, it's critical that the team is not shielded and can take the opportunity to inspect and adapt. Not everything has to go through you before it gets to the Team. It's okay to protect them, but it's not okay to smother them.

Everyone gets a Trophy
Whether you agree with this philosophy in youth sports or not, it most definitely does NOT apply to Scrum. It's important to remember that the

Developers succeed or fail as a team. If one person fails, the Team fails. And that's okay. The team doesn't need to get a trophy every time, or get taken out for ice cream. It's important that you do everything reasonable to keep the team from failing, but when they DO fail (and they will), it's equally important to let it happen and use that failure as a jumping off point in the Retrospective. Failure is an amazing inspect and adapt opportunity, and you should use it to its fullest.

It's important to note that when the team is performing well, hitting all of their commitments, and functioning at a very high level, we recognize that as well. Celebrate with the team when a celebration is called for! Recognize that it's okay to fail, but don't dwell on only the failures. Talk about the positives and congratulate the team!

On the flip side of over-nurturing our teams, we have the person who is perhaps a little TOO passionate about things.

Mistakes happen
Re-read the bit about everyone gets a trophy and remember that it's okay to fail. This is so important that I'm already reiterating it! It's so incredibly easy to personalize things when they go wrong. When a mistake happens (and they will!), don't get upset. This is not an affront to you or to the process. It's not some kind of performance indicator as to how you are doing as Scrum Master. It's just a mistake. Getting mad at the Developers, at the Product Owner, or at yourself will not fix it. Instead, this is your time to coach the team on identifying the problem, and taking steps to avoid it going forward.

X – Scrum Myths Addressed

Common Myth-Conceptions

In this section, we will be talking about some common misunderstandings regarding the role of the Scrum Master. Some misconceptions, or Myth-conceptions, if you will forgive me the pun. I use that because that's exactly what these are; Myths. They have arisen over time and taken on a life of their own. So, it's important that we understand what these various myths are, and how to check them against reality. I guarantee that you will come across one of these myths; whether as a Scrum Master, or in your role working with your Scrum Master, and that's okay. What's important is that we understand them, and can help resolve them so that our teams are functioning at their most efficient.

Now, it's important to note that none of these come from a bad place, or from a desire to simply add more work to the Scrum Master. No, most often these come from a simple place. It's hard to get what it is that the Scrum Master does; it is NOT a traditional IT role, just as Scrum itself is not a traditional IT methodology. When we look at a traditional methodology, such as waterfall, it's really easy to draw lines to the other two roles. In fact, let's do that really quickly.

It's very easy to understand what the Developers do. They write code. That code turns into an increment of software, which we release to our customers. We add value, our customers are delighted, they pay us money, and we are all very happy. It's a win-win. Developers have always been developers. They are awesome at what they do, and we love them for it.

The Product Owner role is similarly easy to understand. He or she is responsible for prioritizing work, and turning that into a well-refined Product Backlog. Our Product Owners are there to make sure that the Developers are working on the right things, at the right time. This is awesome. We don't want our Developers wasting their time working on software that nobody wants or needs.

The Developers and the Product Owner create tangible outcomes. For the developers, it's the increment, and for the PO it is the Product Backlog. As Scrum Masters, what we create is largely intangible, and therein lies the problem. There becomes an assumption that anything not explicitly defined as belonging to the Developers or Product Owner MUST therefore be part of the Scrum Masters job. That's simply not true.

Now, some of these myths derive from other frameworks. These were built on earlier versions of the Scrum Guide, on a misreading of Scrum, or on the skeleton of Scrum without diving into the Scrum Guide. The Scrum Guide itself has evolved over the years, with the November 2020 version having actually purged a lot of the noise that had crept in during previous iterations.

Some of these have come about purely because Scrum Masters have had the bandwidth to do extra work beyond what is in the role's description. If you have that extra capacity, and can take extra steps to help your team, this is awesome. I love this. What happens, however, is that when people become used to the Scrum Master simply doing that work, they transition to another team and are now shocked when the Scrum Master isn't automatically doing it. If you are wearing multiple hats - such as Developer and Scrum Master - you may find you cannot take on this additional work. If you are working with multiple teams, as I am, it is similarly difficult.

Some of this, sadly, just comes from bad Scrum Masters. They exist. We want GREAT Scrum Masters. A great Scrum Master is able to improve the efficiency and outputs of his or her team exponentially, and that's why we are here, right? I want to give you all the tools to be a truly great Scrum Master.

So, let's look at the myths and understand each one.

Myth #1: The Scrum Master runs ALL of the Scrum Team's meetings.

No. We don't.
We are required to facilitate MOST of the Scrum Events, and by most, it turns out I mean some. Let's take a look at how we interact with each of the Events. For the Sprint itself, there is no facilitation required. This is a container event that simply holds the rest of the Events and requires the Roles and Artifacts to be in place. We don't need to do anything more than make sure everything is working.

The first and last events of the Sprint - Sprint Planning and the Sprint Retrospective - we are <u>absolutely</u> required to facilitate. For Sprint Planning, we need to be there to help negotiate scope between the Product Owner and the Developers, to make sure that we have a clearly defined Sprint Backlog that sets our Developers up for success. We'll talk more about this in a bit. For the Sprint Retrospective, it is our job to set the stage, to make sure that our Scrum Teams have a sense of Team Safety, and are able to talk openly and honestly about what happened during the Sprint — good and bad. Without this Transparency, we cannot effectively Inspect and Adapt. We want to make sure that we come out of the Retrospective with a clear action item; something we can do right away in the new Sprint that will improve the way we work. This is critical.

The Sprint Review is a little different. We <u>might</u> be asked to facilitate. Again, this is likely little more than setting the stage for the event, and turning it over to the Product Owner and the Developers to do the actual review with our stakeholders. As the ones closest to the product, they are in the best position to showcase what we did in the Sprint, collect feedback, and turn that feedback into a meaningful plan going forward.

The Daily Scrum is unique, in that we are not actually required for any part of the event. Our job is simply to make sure that the Daily Scrum takes place; every day, at the same time, and ideally within the 15-minute time box. But what if we have a new team, or a team that is relatively immature on their Agile journey? Well, then we are absolutely going to have to step in and facilitate the DSM. We need to coach and teach our Developers how to have an effective Daily Scrum; that answering the dreaded Three Questions is not necessarily the best way to proceed. Once they have it? We can step back and just listen.

Any other meetings that are not Scrum Events, we are just part of the Scrum Team. There are a couple of exceptions that we WILL be required to facilitate, but we will talk about that later in this course.

Myth #2: The Scrum Master is responsible for the board and keeping it up to date.

Not really. The Scrum Team is responsible for the board, and while yes that does include the Scrum Master, we are not the so-called JIRA police. Yes, we are using Azure DevOps, but the concept is the same. When you look at the artifacts, this makes sense. The Product Backlog and Product Goal are owned by the Product Owner, and the Sprint Backlog and Sprint Goal are owned by the Developers. We don't own either of these major artifacts that live on our boards. No, instead what we are responsible for is making sure that the right people are managing the right parts of the application, and are accountable for that work.

We want our Developers, for example, to be managing their User Stories and Tasks as they are creating code for the product. As they finish a task, we want it updated, and the User Story should reflect its accurate, current state at all times. Ideally, this is done in as close to real time as possible, but as long as it is updated prior to the Daily Scrum, we're probably okay. We certainly want to have an accurate picture before that event, so we are making plans based on our current reality.

We might have to do some occasional cleanup. For example, with one of my teams, I have been known to go in after a release and mark all of the stories that were included in that release as Closed. I don't mind doing this, and I took this work upon myself because I wanted to be certain that our board reflected reality. Normally, this task would fall to the Product Owner, or his or her proxy. But honestly, it's easy, and I don't mind it one bit.

Myth #3: The Scrum Master is responsible for generating reports and metrics for the team.

Once again, not really. The Scrum Team should be self-managing. As before, YES, this includes us as Scrum Masters, but that doesn't mean we are the only ones generating information. If someone comes to you with a request for data, by all means provide assistance if you have the bandwidth! We should be doing this when we are able to. But instead of being the point person for all information, we should be looking to turn things around. Create a shared query to drive that data, and take it back to the requestor. Show them how to edit and maintain the query you created, such that they can get this same, or updated, information as they need it moving forward. Rarely do we have a one-off request that will never be needed again.

When it comes to Dashboards, it's slightly more complicated. Again, these are based on Shared Queries in ADO and we should be following the same procedures, but typically, we will have several dashboards to give us a quick HUD of things that are meaningful to us. We will dive a little deeper into dashboards later in this course.

Myth #4: The Scrum Master serves as the "Scrum Police"

Okay, this one we kind of created ourselves. When we came out of traditional command-and-control methodologies (such as waterfall) we were used to having this type of policing somewhere in the organization. As people were tapped to become Scrum Masters — often without training — they brought this structure with them. Sadly, this is wrong. We don't have the power to outright tell our teams what to do, how to do it, or anything of the sort. The only thing we have control of, remember, is the PROCESS. The Developers own the HOW, and the Product Owner owns the WHAT. As long as the 3-5-3 stricture of Scrum (3 roles, 5 events, and 3 artifacts) is in place, the team is free to experiment within that structure. We WANT them to and should be encouraging them at every turn.

If the team comes to us and says "Hey, we don't think we need to do a Sprint Review, it doesn't add anything and is a waste of our time," we should be stepping in and saying "No." In this case, it's on us to explain to the team why this is important and what value we add by having this Event. It probably is an indicator that we need to take a stronger role in setting it up and/or facilitating the event. But because we own the Process of Scrum, we have this authority. It's our job to make sure Scrum is well understood and all of the pieces are in place and effective.

Myth #5: The Scrum Master is the person who removes all impediments for the team.

Close, but not quite.

The Scrum Master helps cause the removal of impediments. See the slight difference there? It's a key one. We aren't the people actively running around and removing every single impediment from the team. There often simply isn't enough time. Instead, we want to coach our teams on how to remove impediments themselves where possible. Often, this is as simple as copying us on an email thread. The recipient will see that we are now on the thread and actively watching, and will take action. If not, we are now in a position to follow up accordingly, using our people skills to foster good communication, and demonstrating to our Scrum Teams how to proceed in the future. Lead by example.

Again, we want our Scrum Teams - and specifically our Developers - to be self-managing, not relying on us every time they hit the smallest of roadblocks.

Myth #6: The Scrum Master is the Leader of the Scrum Team

Myth #7: The Scrum Master is a servant to the Scrum Team.

These two myths go hand in hand. Why? Because of the phrase "servant-leader." There's a very good reason it was dropped in the Scrum Guide! It is a hard thing for some people to fully grasp. We are absolutely here to help serve our Scrum Teams in any way we can. That's part of our job. And yet we are also here to act as a guide: to the Developers, the Product Owner, and the Organization & Enterprise. It's a unique role that serves a very specific purpose within the Organization as a whole.

The truth is that we have a HUGE amount of power, while maintaining absolutely none. Nobody reports to us. We don't tell people what to do. But when it comes to the process of Scrum, nobody wields more authority. We just use it in ways that people don't expect, through coaching, mentoring, and teaching. We lead by example, remaining calm in the face of chaos, and act as a reassuring voice to the team that things are going to be okay. We are a cheerleader when the team needs one, and the person who says "that's okay" when something goes wrong. Our influence over the Scrum Team is enormous.

Myth #8: The Scrum Master is not as important as the Product Owner.

This is completely incorrect. The Scrum Master is a critical role on the Scrum Team; in fact, you can't have a Scrum Team without one. All three roles are required. This makes sense. It's a triangle, the strongest structure there is. In fact, the Scrum Master's power helps to offset that of the Product Owner and maintain a balance.

The Product Owner is always being coached by the Scrum Master, even when he or she doesn't realize it. This is probably happening all the time. That's cool. We don't need to set up explicit coaching sessions for our POs. We lead by what we do and how we work. We respect the Product Owner's knowledge and appreciate their guidance. In many cases, we actually report directly to our Product Owner. A good PO knows this is a two-way street and that we are leading them, as much as they are leading us.

As a Scrum Master, you also help protect the team against an overzealous Product Owner. Remember that the Product Owner is a value maximizer, and wants to get as much possible value into each Sprint, and therefore each increment, as possible. We are there to serve as a buffer, to make sure that the team has the RIGHT amount of work that they are capable of completing within the Sprint. We do this by using Velocity and Capacity to understand what our teams can achieve, and sticking within those boundaries.

XI - Distribution Problems

This is all Great, but...

If you have the first edition of this book, you might recall that this used to be a section in the final chapter. Thanks for buying that first edition, by the way! That first edition was published in January 2020, and of course, the whole world changed two months later. We went from going to the office every day, to everyone working remotely almost overnight. This chapter emerged from the new reality, as it became immediately apparent that this topic warranted much greater detail than it first had.

If you've been paying attention to the book thus far, you might have noticed that many of the things I have written imply an "in-office" situation. Many of us are not back there, or never will be. COVID taught us that knowledge work, such as software development, can all be done remotely with no loss of productivity. The skills we require just need to Adapt. Hey wait, that's one of the pillars of Scrum!

Scrum works best with teams that are co-located. Face-to-face communication is important. But that's not the world we all live in these days. Some of you may be back in a traditional office environment. Awesome, I hope you are thriving and can take everything in this book to this point and make it happen. Some people, myself included, want no part of ever stepping into an office again. That two hours I used to spend commuting every day are now spent playing with my dog, or getting an extra ½ hour of sleep in the morning. I consider myself fortunate.

What Is Our New Reality, Exactly?

The reality of our modern workplace is that we are likely to have distributed teams, whether it is simply people working remotely for a day, or a global workforce that is located around the world. This was becoming reality long before COVID changed everything. Handling a distributed Scrum Team presents its own set of unique challenges and issues we have to face to succeed. The decision to distribute teams needs to be well thought-out and the challenges and risks need to be understood.

Things already discussed in this book become even more important once the Developers are distributed. Having a clearly defined Definition of Done, and standards around engineering practices that are fully understood by all team members is imperative. You cannot allow quality to slip just because the team is not in the same place. Making sure that everyone understands how defects will be handled in real-time takes on a new importance. Solid practices of TDD, pair programming, and continuous integration help ensure the team's success.

When the team is typically co-located but dealing with someone - or the entire team - working remotely, these factors all come into play. The team should function in exactly the same way they would if they were at their desks.

Many, if not most, of our organizations now are also working with an offshore workforce. I have worked with engineers around the globe -- in Ukraine, Russia, Lebanon, India, China and more -- as well as collaborated with team members working offshore in Guam and American Samoa. How do we apply the same practices we have in the office to a globally distributed team and expect the same results?

One of the earliest factors that comes into play is resolving any possibility of an "us vs. them" mentality. Members of both your offshore team and your local team will likely have baggage from a previous distributed experience, and biases that come with that baggage. This may have built up a sense of mistrust that needs to be resolved immediately. Talking about old experiences openly and early in the process will go a long way toward resolving these differences. The other immediately noticeable issue is dealing with the time difference. One or more members of your team, whether local or remote, may need to adjust their schedule to allow for some degree of overlap in the day. The Daily Scrum, once held in the morning, may now be held at the end of the day. Sprint Planning, Review, and Retrospective events may need to shift in time to allow all required members to attend. Your schedule needs to be as agile as your team.

Where possible, encourage pair programming between developers in disparate locations to build a sense of camaraderie and break down some of the barriers. Find ways to get remote team members to swarm around common work.

Cultural differences present another potential trouble spot for the team. If remote team members are accustomed to being told what to do, making them feel empowered to work freely on any available work in the Sprint Backlog can be a challenge. I have seen an issue with Sprint Planning where when asked to estimate a PBI, the remote team members would go on mute and discuss it amongst themselves and then come back on and all vote identically. Switching from a phone call to a video chat eliminated this. Use video chat for your Daily Scrum Meeting, and require that everyone who is on the call have their video turned on. You can instantly see who is paying attention and who is distracted, just as you would with everyone in the same room. Use an online Planning Poker tool during estimation, combined with the video call, so you can see that everyone is estimating independently.

Try swapping roles on the team. Have one of the remote workers facilitate the team's Sprint Retrospective. Ask open-ended questions and foster an environment where everyone is feeling safe and empowered. These things will help break down cultural barriers.

Ultimately, there is a common theme to many of the problems with a distributed team, and it all comes down to communication. We live in an age where we all have instant communication devices at our fingertips almost 24/7. Make the most of the tools available to you to foster excellent and open communication. The challenges are still very real, and will have to be overcome, but simply making sure that the entire team is able to communicate at any time, about any issue they are facing, will go a long way toward solving any problems that arise.

Better Ways of Communicating

Fortunately, we have ways to get us through the perils of distribution! We are software people, and there is software designed for just this purpose!

Clearly having a first-class communication tool that allows the team to chat, share their screens, and video conference as needed becomes vital. Having a digital tool to manage your Product and Sprint Backlogs is required, as not everyone can see sticky notes on the wall somewhere. In fact, I have a box full of unused sticky notes that I simply don't need anymore.

Tools like Slack, Microsoft Teams, and others allow instant communication among Scrum Team members, whether in dedicated channels or 1:1. Zoom became the most downloaded application in the world almost overnight in 2020. Use it, or a similar video-conferencing tool to your advantage. Cameras ON should always be the default. Don't let someone turn their camera off and come back unless they're actually having connectivity issues. Remember not everyone's connection is created equal, especially in a global workforce. If you join a team that typically runs with cameras off, turn yours on and lead by example. Just because the team isn't face-to-face doesn't mean we shouldn't be able to see one another. That simple act helps build camaraderie. It's great to see everyone smiling during your Daily Scrum!

The days of using painter's tape and sticky notes to track our Sprint have come and gone. We are all using a tool like Jira, Rally, Azure DevOps or others to help us keep track of our Sprints. We use the built in Kanban board to help drive discussion in the Daily Scrum, and the Backlog to help us during Sprint Planning (and Refinement). We use the concept of Epics, Features and PBIs (or User Stories) within the tool to help us organize our work and provide us with a way to have meaningful discussions around that work.

Remember that most impediments are fundamentally communication issues. By helping the organization implement great ways of communicating remotely, we can eliminate a great majority of these impediments before they even happen.

There are digital tools to assist with every aspect of Scrum, from using communication tools during the Daily Scrum, to digital boards designed to help us facilitate a Sprint Retrospective. Find the tools that you like and

USE THEM. If pricing is an issue, be prepared to make a case for the tool of your choice to the organization. A truly Agile organization will make sure you have the tools to succeed!

I will say that I still have a whiteboard near my desk for day-to-day notes, and I maintain a personal Trello board to help me keep track of my own PBIs across teams. I have been known to spend hours on Slack with one of my POs, where we are often brainstorming ideas on how to make key process improvements that will benefit the whole Scrum Team.

What Else Can We Do?

Some other great practices have come up with my Scrum Teams to increase focus and produce maximum value. One of my teams has a strict "no meeting Friday" rule in effect. We conduct the Daily Scrum asynchronously via Slack. Another team uses the Daily Scrum time on Friday for game time, and fostering team building.

One of the side effects of being wholly distributed is that meetings become more prominent and important to some people, as they need to know information that they can't get by just walking over to your board and looking at sticky notes, or coming to your desk to ask questions. Avoid unnecessary meetings at all costs. If weekly "status" meetings are a thing, see if you can find a way to distribute that status electronically and cancel the weekly meetings. Get time back for your Product Owner and your Developers any way you can so they can create value. Remember that Focus is one of our Scrum Values, and we need to promote that as much as possible. Having recently done this, I can say it was well received by most people, and they are now quite happy knowing that they will get their status at the same time every week, without having to spend time in a meeting that may accomplish nothing.

We can't take the team out for ice cream anymore, because it would melt during the delivery process. But what we can do is have a virtual happy hour on Zoom! Everyone grabs the beverage of your choice (no judgment) and spend an hour every so often just sitting and chatting as a team, with no particular goal in mind. The only rule is no talking about work! Hit a huge milestone in your project? Have cookies delivered to everyone! Get t-shirts printed and send them to the members of your team. I guarantee they will proudly wear them. Form a book club on the team and pick a great technical book to read and discuss together. Team building is even more important when we can't all get together around the proverbial water cooler anymore. Get creative!

Remember the quote from Ken Schwaber earlier in this book? Scrum can become even more disruptive in a distributed team. Actively seek ways to smooth things out and allow your Scrum Teams to be the awesome teams you know they are.

XII - Leveling Up: Ding!

Agility Stability

One of the ways we can make sure that our Agile efforts succeed is to build stable high-performing teams. Constantly changing our team makeup leads to increased instability and slows down productivity and reduces the amount of value our teams can deliver. Sometimes, we have no choice but to stand up a brand-new team, but often it's easier and more productive to move work to an existing team than to break teams up and form new ones.

Tuckman's model of group development, first introduced in 1965, states that teams need to go through four stages to mature: Forming, Storming, Norming, and Performing. If we are always reforming our teams, we necessarily reset the model back to the first stage, and we fail to realize the final Performing stage to its fullest. Furthermore, when we have a stable team, it becomes increasingly important that we allow that team to focus on exactly one product. The less time the team spends that is dedicated to a single product, the less the team is able to deliver. Dedicated teams deliver value at twice the rate of teams that are working across multiple products.

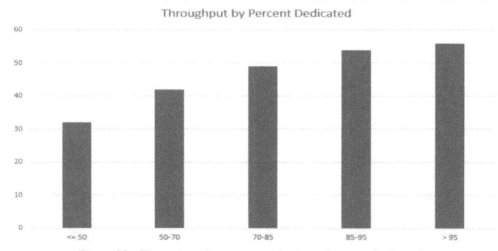

Figure 29 - Throughput increases as the team is more dedicated

170

Adding a person to an existing team, even if they are already fully dedicated, begins the forming process anew. Worse, when we look at the number of communication pathways that are in place as we build teams, that number grows greatly as we add people to the team. Team PAWS has a total of five Engineers, plus the Scrum Master and Product Owner. Alone, the five-member team has a total of 10 communication paths. As a full Scrum team, that number jumps up to 21. The team recognizes that they need one more person, and Maria joins the team, bringing with her a strong technical writing background and outstanding leadership skills. She jumps in willingly and starts working with Team PAWS from Day One. The team's velocity slows down as a result. Why?

The mere act of onboarding a new person takes time. There is training to be considered as Maria ramps up on what Team PAWS has been doing. She needs to learn the team and what the team's norms are, and the rest of the team has to adapt to having her presence as well. The communication pathways similarly take a hit. Now the Developers alone goes from 10 to 15 pathways, and the entire Scrum team jumps from 21 to 28! Every person and every pathway we add to the team presents a communication challenge, as we must make sure that everyone is in the loop at all times. If we jump our Developers for Team PAWS to the recommended maximum of nine, we are looking at 36 pathways for the team and 55 for the entire Scrum Team. That's a lot of chances for things to be missed if we are not diligent.

N (N - 1) / 2 COMMUNICATION PATHWAYS

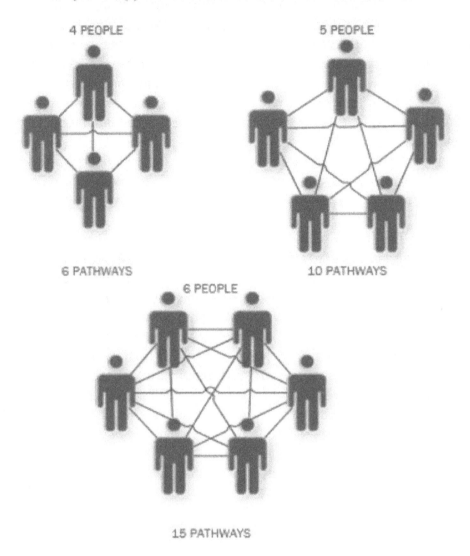

4 PEOPLE

5 PEOPLE

6 PATHWAYS

10 PATHWAYS

6 PEOPLE

15 PATHWAYS

Figure 30 - Communication Pathways increase as people are added to the team

Keeping our teams small and stable goes a long way toward increasing our agility. Stable teams result in up to 60% improved productivity and 40% improved predictability[xix]. Teams in the recommended range of 3-9 yield the greatest balance of quality, productivity, and predictability. Keep your teams as stable as possible and move work to the teams rather than forming teams for the work, and you will see the maximum benefit.

Applied Modifiers

Sometimes circumstances will arise that will make someone say "This isn't working. We should change how we do Scrum." This should raise a huge red flag. The best advice when someone wants to modify Scrum itself is this: don't. Instead of modifying Scrum, use this as a chance to ask important questions about what is actually happening and why there appears to be a need to change things. Remember the chess analogy used earlier; if you change the rules, you are now doing something else. Don't be in a "Scrum, but..." organization unless it is absolutely unavoidable.

Normally, when someone wants to modify Scrum itself, there are one or more pain points that make them feel like such a change is necessary. Finding what those pain points are can be difficult, but will get you into a position to determine the root cause and act on that instead. Often, it's the transparency that Scrum demands because of the empirical process. People can feel exposed and uncomfortable. This is normal. This becomes especially challenging in organizations where silos have been allowed to develop. Teams that exist in silos tend to not like the idea of allowing others to see what is happening behind the curtain. There is fear of being judged, of being confronted, or just of admitting that things might not be as great as they want you to believe. Transparency opens us up to exposure to our peers and requires accountability. This is a great thing.

If you hear things like "That's not how we do things" or "That's out of our control" you can be assured that you have a problem with transparency. Rather than changing Scrum, figure out how you can make these teams more comfortable with how increased transparency helps them, not hurts them. Scrum is not a framework that allows you to continue working as before. The status quo will be challenged, if not outright torn down. Ask the team what they would do if there were no such restrictions and allow them to dream big. Then try to remove the often-artificial constraints that prevent them from living in that world. Change is hard and makes people uncomfortable. Being Agile makes us embrace change and live comfortably in the chaos. Scrum requires our time, our focus, and our dedication to make it succeed. This is hard work, and it's very easy to fall back on old habits when things don't work the way we hoped.

Look to see that the Scrum roles are properly filled and that the people filling those roles are doing so effectively. Check the Scrum events; are they effective, or are the Scrum Teams merely going through the motions? Look at the Product Backlog and Sprint Backlogs to see that Backlog Items are well-defined and well-refined. Check to see that the Scrum Team is actively engaging in the cycle of Inspect and Adapt. Find where there are issues with executing the basic 3-5-3 structure of Scrum and coach the team through the weak spots. Coach the team on the Scrum Values and why they are important.

Rather than modifying Scrum, use the knowledge you gain from asking difficult questions to modify how your teams are working. Scrum is intended to be a strong framework, with the pillars of empiricism holding it firmly in place. When you start to change things, you change the very foundation of how your team functions. Changing Scrum introduces instability that you can't always recognize right away. It will create a weakness in your teams at best, and will cause the entire thing to crumble to the ground at worst.

Hitting the Scales

At some point in many organizations, there comes a time when the need to scale your Scrum effort will arise. A quick search for how to scale Scrum will result in several different approaches/frameworks. Without touching Google, I can come up with at least six off the top of my head, and I have hands-on experience with most. I don't want to do a deep dive into any of them. There are excellent resources on each of the various scaling frameworks out there that can cover them in the proper amount of detail. Rather, it's important to think about what we are trying to gain by scaling Scrum, and the potential pitfalls of doing so.

Even the most cursory look at how to scale Scrum will show you some important things:

- Scrum itself lies at the heart of how most scaling frameworks operate.
- There is no single, universally-recognized way to scale Scrum.
- There is a fair amount of overlap in the various frameworks, but the terminology varies greatly.

I can't (and don't want to) endorse any single framework. If your organization is having a discussion about how to scale Scrum, it's important that you look at all of the options and see what is going to fit best within your organization. A consultant hired to assist you with scaling Scrum almost certainly comes in with a framework already in mind and will invariably lead you down their chosen path. That is their job. That path might be the right one for them, but NOT the right one for you. The more research you do into the various scaling frameworks the better.

Read what makes each framework unique. While each scaling framework has the same goal, how they go about attaining said goal will vary. The terminology will not be the same, even when talking about essentially the same event or artifact. The number of additional roles may be increased, although ultimately everyone is still either a Scrum Master, Product Owner, or Developer, just functioning at different layers in the organization. How the roles function may change depending on where they are organizationally. Ask yourself if you have the structure already in place, or if you are making radical changes just for the sake of change. Think about the existing structure in your organization and how a new framework would cause your structure to change.

Scrum is hard. Scaling Scrum compounds those problems and exposes even more pain points in your organization. It requires a full buy-in from upper management on down or it will not work. Just having a Scrum of Scrums alone is not enough to start scaling, although it is certainly an important step. The Scrum framework is, without changing a thing, designed to handle complex products. Trying to scale it up will invariably introduce additional complexity and may not provide additional value. Sometimes just having strong and stable Scrum teams working on their products is enough. Know what you are trying to gain by scaling and have a clear goal in mind before you even begin the conversation and select a framework. The time you spend up front will help you realize the value at the end.

I have seen Scrum scaled up successfully, and while it took some time for everything to click, it worked. I have also seen it fall apart the moment those who championed it left the organization, and even successful Scrum Teams were left struggling to find their place. I have seen how different methods of scaling can achieve the same result, given the will to change and empowerment of those trying to drive that change. I have seen silos torn down as teams are forced to work together on a common product from a common Product Backlog, and communication channels open up. I have also seen silos reinforced as teams were more protective of their territory and did not want to try a new way of working.

Just as you need to choose what is right for your team when it comes to scaling, you need to know your organization and what the needs are before you try introducing additional complexity. Ask a lot of questions and understand the challenges, and you will be able to successfully find a way to scale that will bring maximum value to your organization.

A final word on scaling: as I indicated previously there are several published ways to scale Agile/Scrum. At least one of them does not rely on the Scrum Guide as its basis, and has changed the rules of the game to suit its purposes. In fact, the creators of Scrum – Jeff Sutherland and Ken Schwaber – have come up with wholly separate methods by which to do so. If they can't agree on the right way, perhaps there is no universal answer to this question. Do what is right for YOUR organization.

Lean-ing into Change

Lean thinking is an important part of being Agile, and the definition of Scrum (see above   !) refers to lean thinking as part of the whole. But what is lean thinking, exactly? Well, the whole idea of lean comes -

unsurprisingly - from manufacturing, and from the Toyota Production System (TPS) in particular. But how do manufacturing principles apply to the world of software engineering and knowledge work?

Frankly, lean as a whole would take an entire book to translate into software development, and that book has been written. But let's dig into the principles of Lean, how they apply to our world, and really dive into the single most important thing(s) we can do to make our organizations leaner in nature.

Ohno-san

If this is your first time looking at how Agile ultimately ties back to manufacturing, and TPS in particular, let's take a step back and look at this. Taiichi Ohno is considered the father of the Toyota Production System, which completely turned the world of manufacturing upside-down.

Ohno-san was born in 1912, and started to come up with what ultimately became TPS in the 1950s. The ultimate key to TPS was to put quality before anything else, which directly translates to one of the lean principles we will get to shortly. It was through aggressive attention to quality and the elimination of waste that TPS threw the world of manufacturing as we know it into the 20th century.

Ohno is also known for his "Ten Precepts" to think and act to win:

- You are a cost. First reduce waste.
- First say, "I can do it." And try before everything.
- The workplace is a teacher. You can find answers only in the workplace.
- Do anything immediately. Starting something right now is the only way to win.
- Once you start something, persevere with it. Do not give up until you finish it.
- Explain difficult things in an easy-to-understand manner. Repeat things that are easy to understand.
- Waste is hidden. Do not hide it. Make problems visible.

- Valueless motions are equal to shortening one's life.
- Re-improve what was improved for further improvement.
- Wisdom is given equally to everybody. The point is whether one can exercise it.
-

If you're paying attention, you can see more than one parallel to the Agile Manifesto, or to the principles of Scrum right there. Yep, this all comes from manufacturing. Ohno-san changed the world after WWII, and the precepts he touted still hold true.

Principally speaking

So, at its core, lean software comes down to a simple set of principles. Let's take a quick look:

- Eliminate waste
- Amplify learning
- Decide as late as possible
- Deliver as fast as possible
- Empower the team
- Build integrity in
- Optimize the whole

Most of these don't require a deep dive, at least not where this book is concerned. It's relatively easy, particularly given the context elsewhere, to understand things like "Deliver as fast as possible". We want to get value to our customers rapidly! This shouldn't be a thing we have to think about, and this is part of the proverbial secret sauce that gives Scrum a huge advantage over waterfall, or any other traditional project management techniques

Where we can really dig in and gain deeper understanding is that first bullet. Eliminate waste. What is it we mean exactly, and how does that translate into knowledge work?

Waste not!

So how, exactly do we define waste? This, again, comes from TPS, with tweaks made to accommodate the current world, and software development in particular. The core principles behind eliminating waste come down to this:

- Partially done work
- Extra features
- Relearning
- Task switching
- Waiting
- Handoffs
- Defects

None of these, by themselves are difficult to understand, but when we start to Optimize the Whole, they become more challenging. Let's go ahead and take a look at each waste in turn and understand what's there.

Partially Done Work

In manufacturing, this would be considered Inventory; the single greatest waste of all. In the software engineering world, this waste is any code that isn't working as described in the PBI and/or isn't checked in. Code that only works on the developer's computer is absolutely partially done. Code that doesn't have unit tests associated with it (in accordance with the team's DoD) is another excellent example. The clear point here is that partially done work adds absolutely no value, and is a massive waste.

Extra Features

The opposite of partially done work, is work we've done that nobody asked us for. If it isn't in the PBI, there may be a VERY good reason for that. Developers should not anticipate "they're going to want this" and just go ahead and write it. At the very least, check with the PO before writing that code. It may be that she opted to exclude that from a release, or that the customer isn't particularly interested in that right now. Any code we write that doesn't match the PBI adds overhead we don't want to carry.

Relearning

We've all been here. Remember that code a Developer wrote last year and hasn't touched since? Hey, it's time to make a change to that. How long will it take to ramp back up on that? Even the most beautifully written code will take a little time to relearn. Time spent not adding value is time wasted. We can't eliminate this waste, but we want to do everything within our power to minimize it. Writing great code the first time makes this waste more manageable.

Task Switching
We've already covered the costs and wastes incurred by context switching. Try to remain 100% on a task until it's complete.

Waiting / Handoffs
We can't do very much about this one. Sometimes we have a dependency on another team before we are able to move forward. Their timeline is obviously out of our control. What we CAN do is call out dependencies as early as possible, and get them on the other team's backlog long before we need it. If we wait until the last second to say "we need this you guys," we can't expect them to drop everything and prioritize our work. The best we can hope for is in their next Sprint.

Handoffs may be unavoidable also, depending on your system architecture. If something needs to go through another team at some point before it can be released, you have a handoff. Every time one of these hits, you incur waste, because waiting is now GOING to happen. Again, we can't eliminate these, but we can try to mitigate them.

Defects
Well, this one is obvious, right? Our Developers all write perfect bug-free code the first time, so we don't have to worry about defects! Don't we all wish that were true. Code is complex, and bugs sneak in from time to time. Hopefully we find them during development when they are exponentially cheaper to fix. But every defect we find requires rework, and possibly relearning. I can't tell your Developers to just write better code, but this is still a waste you need to be highly aware of. Drive that defect rate down through better unit testing and amazing automated testing by your QE Developers.

Hard Work is Hard

Whither Certifications?

A quick look around will show you any number of various certifications for Scrum. Whether you are a Scrum Master, a Product Owner, or one of the Developers, there are certifications for you. I have mine, and I am proud of every one of them. This book is not a study guide for any single certification available, though there have been parts that would certainly help you, if that is your goal. If you are looking for a new opportunity, having one or more certifications may help you get your foot in the door.

Ultimately, I view all of my certifications as investments in myself, and every certification exam I have taken has been with that in mind. I am not going to endorse any particular certification or certifying body as being superior to another. I have taken the exams I have to this point for very specific reasons. Primarily, I view certification as a means to test myself and validate that I have learned the knowledge required. Your certification is important, but choose the path you do for good reasons. Some only require that you attend a specific course with no exam, others only require that you have practical knowledge from experience. Some require a recurring fee, others do not. Some require that you maintain continuous learning as you move forward in your career to show that you are always honing your skills, others are for life. The path you choose in certifying is a personal one.

The dark side of certification is that for some people, having those letters after your name is everything. Passing the exam does not always mean you have mastered the material. I have seen certifications used -- and abused -- in this way far too many times. I have interviewed candidates for a position whose knowledge of Scrum falls apart under the slightest bit of scrutiny, but who proudly claim that they are certified and therefore more than qualified to hold the position. I have seen Scrum Masters who are output-driven project managers, and Product Owners who know nothing of their product, but all whom carry sets of letters after their names and will proudly exclaim that they are certified. I have seen a group of people all sitting in one room taking the exact same certification exam and discussing the best answer amongst themselves, and then proudly wearing their newly gained certification. Having a PMP is amazing, but does not fit in the world of Scrum.

Certification should not be an end goal, but a possible step on your continuing journey to become more Agile. Find the ones that best suit you and go for it should you choose to do so. Prove to yourself and your peers that you know the material, and back up that certification with your actions. Apply the knowledge you have gained in ways that will help drive your team forward. Certifications are awesome, and I am proud of mine, but the ultimate validation is how your team performs and the value they create. Everything else is just a bonus.

Work Your Ticket

If any of you have experience as a Cub Scout or Boy Scout leader, you might have heard this expression before. If you have taken Wood Badge, you recognize it well and are probably now humming *Back to Gilwell* (for the record, I used to be a Beaver). For those who don't get the reference at all, it's pretty simple.

Wood Badge is the ultimate in Scout Leader training. It's an intense seven days that leaves you completely exhausted and empowered. It is a full week (or three weekends) of nonstop training that challenges you at every step and brings out the best in everyone. I saw an entire group of men and women visibly crying and hugging each other at the end of the week because we were sad it was over, despite being completely sleep-deprived. At every critical juncture in training, you add to your "ticket". Your ticket lists specific actions you are going to take to apply the knowledge you have just learned when you return to "normal" life. You own your ticket. You work with your counselor to get everything done and you have to document every step you take. You have six months to two years to work the ticket to completion and only then do you receive the recognition for all of your hard work. I take great pride in having successfully worked my ticket.

I suggest here that you start writing your own Scrum ticket. Think about the various ideas and concepts you have learned, be it in this book, another book, a class you have taken, or an online resource. Actively seek out new opportunities for learning and carve out time from your already busy schedule to dedicate yourself to learning something new. Come up with some broad categories where you can take actions, and list two or three things you can specifically do with your Scrum Teams starting right now. Don't settle for the easy wins, but challenge yourself. Feel like you can do better with Sprint Planning? Add two or three actions you can take to make your Sprint Planning better. Feel like your Retrospectives lack life and energy? Commit yourself to coming up with a new game or a different way to facilitate the event.

Hold yourself responsible. Print your ticket out and keep it somewhere you can always see it. As you do everything you committed yourself to, create a printout with any handouts, photographs, or just written out concepts and thoughts you have and keep it in a binder with your printed ticket. Document every step you take and collect it all together. By the time you have done everything, you will have a workbook of your experiences that you can look back on or share with your peers to push them forward as well.

It is not enough just to learn. We must apply what we have learned to truly gain knowledge. Not everything you try will work, and that's okay as long as you learn from that experience. It's vital that we practice what we do with intent and be unafraid to try new things. When you are pushing yourself and your team forward, be in the moment, actively listening and participating in whatever you are doing. This is not the time to be a passive coach.

Speaking of coaches; get one. It might be a peer or your immediate supervisor. Ask him or her to sit in on some of the activities and events you are facilitating and give honest feedback. A good coach will both support you and challenge you, providing a new perspective you may not otherwise see. The coach will help to hold you accountable. Your coach will help you break free of beliefs that are limiting you and push you to expand your horizons. Feedback is not limited to your coach. Don't be afraid to ask your team how you are doing. Get their input on the work you are doing for them and with them, and the ways they think you can improve. It's important not to take any feedback personally, and not to react to feedback when you get it, whether it's good or bad. Simply listen and accept it, and thank the person(s) giving you feedback for their help. Remember that you are getting their input because you genuinely want to know; you are not looking for validation but for an opportunity to learn and grow in your role. Think with intent about what you have been told and then you can take actions.

Use your ticket as your personal kaizen and push yourself to do everything you have committed yourself to. Expand your boundaries and find the opportunities to grow.

Work Your Ticket.

Acknowledgements

This couldn't have happened without a whole lot of people.

Firstly: To my family, who put up with me when was obsessing over a minute detail, developing anxiety when I was waiting for feedback on my manuscript, and for just being there when I needed you. That happened on many occasions, including a whole bunch when you didn't realize it.

To Sheila Grimes for giving the entire rough manuscript a diligent eye and helping me to clean up so many of the rough edges.

To Christine Grail for giving the whole thing an extra lair of polish, and helping to point out where I could keep refining the work to get it just exactly perfect.

To Sunita Dhungana for being my first beta reader, for all of your support and effort to make me into a great Scrum Master.

To Paul Thomas and Julie Szwaja for all of your unwavering support from the moment I told you I was considering this crazy venture, and for giving pieces of this your once over and feedback from your points of view.

To Anna Pizzoferrato for being a cheerleader when I needed one, and for being a willing sounding board for some of the material that ended up in this book (even when you didn't realize you were doing so!).

To all of the various teams and people I have worked with, you have all made me into the Scrum Professional I am today, and I couldn't have done it without all of you.

Lastly, to Wilson for being the bestest puppy ever and knowing when daddy needed play time or snuggles to de-stress.

References

Adkins, Lyssa. 2010. *Coaching Agile Teams: A Companion for ScrumMasters, Agile Coaches, and Project Managers in Transition.* Addison-Wesley Professional.

Beck, Kent, Mike Beedle, Arie van Bennekum, Alistair Cockburn, Ward Cunningham, Martin Fowler, James Grenning, et al. 2001. *Manifesto for Agile Software Development.* www.agilemanifesto.org.

Caroli, Paulo, and T.C. Caetano. n.d. *The Team Building Prime Directive.* http://www.funretrospectives.com/the-team-building-prime-directive/.

Cohn, Mike. 2017. *Add the Right Amount of Detail to User Stories.* 3 October. https://www.mountaingoatsoftware.com/blog/add-the-right-amount-of-detail-to-user-stories.

—. 2005. *Agile Estimating and Planning.* Prentice Hall.

—. 2019. *An Agile Team Shouldn't Finish Everything Every Iteration.* 19 March. https://www.mountaingoatsoftware.com/blog/an-agile-team-shouldnt-finish-everything-every-iteration.

—. 2017. *How Programmers and Testers (and Others) Should Collaborate on User Stories.* 14 September. https://www.mountaingoatsoftware.com/blog/how-programmers-and-testers-and-others-should-collaborate-on-user-stories.

—. 2018. *Include All Team Members in Sprint Meetings. Yes, Them Too.* 21 February. https://www.mountaingoatsoftware.com/blog/include-all-team-members-in-sprint-meetings.-yes-them-too.

—. 2004. *User Stories Applied: For Agile Software Development.* Addison-Wesley Professional.

—. 2017. *Why the Whole Team Should Participate When Estimating.* 18 July. https://www.mountaingoatsoftware.com/blog/why-the-whole-team-should-participate-when-estimating.

—. 2019. *Your Team Won't Think of Everything in Sprint Planning Meetings. And That's OK.* 30 April. https://www.mountaingoatsoftware.com/blog/your-team-wont-think-of-everything-in-sprint-planning-meetings-and-thats-ok.

Derby, Esther. 2011. *Team Values, Team Norms, Working Agreements, and Rules.* 18 April. https://www.estherderby.com/2011/04/norms-values-working-agreements-simple-rules.html.

Derby, Esther, and Diana Larsen. 2006. *Agile Retrospectives Making Good Teams Great.* Pragmatic Bookshelf.

Goldstein, Ilan. 2016. *Scrum Shortcuts Without Cutting Corners: Agile Tactics, Tools, & Tips.* Addison-Wesley.

Jeffries, Ron. 2001. *Essential XP, Card Conversation, Confirmation.* 30 Aug. https://ronjeffries.com/xprog/articles/expcardconversationconfirmation/.

Kerth, Norman L. 2001. *Project Retrospectivers: A Handbook for Team Reviews.* Dorset House.

Maccherone, Larry. 2014. *The Impact of Agile Quantified: A de-Mystery Thriller.* https://submissions.agilealliance.org/system/attachments/attachments/000/000/955/original/Impact_of_Agile_Quantified_2014_edition.pdf.

Ockerman, Stephanie. 2017. *Coaching Secret: Follow the Aliveness.* 26 June. https://www.agilesocks.com/coaching-secrets-follow-aliveness/.

Patton, Jeff, and Peter Economy. 2014. *User Story Mapping.* Sebastolpol, CA: O'Reilly Media Inc.

Pink, Daniel. 2011. *Drive: The Surprising Truth About What Motivates Us.* Riverhead Books.

Rubin, Ken. 2012. *Essential Scrum: A Practical Guide to the Most Popular Agile Process.* Addison-Wesley Professional.

Schwaber, Ken. 2011. *Scrum Fails?* 7 April. https://kenschwaber.wordpress.com/2011/04/07/scrum-fails/.

—. 2006. *Scrum is Hard and Disruptive.*

Schwaber, Ken, and Jeff Sutherland. 2017. *The Scrum Guide.* November. https://scrumguides.org/scrum-guide.html.

Sochova, Zuzana. 2017. *The Great ScrumMaster.* Addison-Wesley Professional.

Sutherland, Jeff. 2003. *SCRUM: Get Your Requirements Straight Before Coding.* March. http://jeffsutherland.org/2003_03_01_oldstuff.html.

Sutherland, Jeff, and J.J. Sutherland. 2014. *Scrum, The Art of Doing Twice the Work in Half the Time.* Currency.

Takeuchi, Hirotaka, and Ikujiro Nonaka. 1986. "The New New Product Development Game." *Harvard Business Review*, January.

Weinberg, Gerald M. 1992. *Quality Software Management: Systems Thinking.* Dorset House.

[i] https://www.scrumguides.org/scrum-guide.html#definition

[ii] https://www.scrumguides.org/scrum-guide.html#values

[iii] https://www.scrumguides.org/scrum-guide.html#values

[iv] https://www.scrumguides.org/scrum-guide.html#values

[v] https://www.scrumguides.org/scrum-guide.html#values

[vi] https://www.scrumguides.org/scrum-guide.html#values

[vii] https://kenschwaber.wordpress.com/2011/04/07/scrum-fails/

[viii] The Team Building Prime Directive

[ix] Hirotaka Takeuchi & Ikujiro Nonaka, The New New Product Development Game, Harvard Business Review, Jan-Feb 1986

[x] Sutherland, Jeff, Scrum, The Art of Doing Twice the Work in Half the Time, p. 5

[xi] Jeffries, Ron, Essential XP: Card, Conversation, Confirmation

[xii] Sutherland, Jeff -- SCRUM: Get Your Requirements Straight Before Coding

[xiii] https://www.mountaingoatsoftware.com/blog/an-agile-team-shouldnt-finish-everything-every-iteration

[xiv] Kerth, Norm, Project Retrospectives: A Handbook for Team Review

[xv] http://scrumguides.org/scrum-guide.html#team-sm

[xvi] Weinberg, Gerald M., Quality Software Management: Systems Thinking, p. 284

[xvii] https://www.estherderby.com/2011/04/norms-values-working-agreements-simple-rules/

[xviii] https://www.agilesocks.com/coaching-secrets-follow-aliveness

[xix] The Impact of Agile Quantified

www.ingramcontent.com/pod-product-compliance
Lightning Source LLC
Chambersburg PA
CBHW051051050326
40690CB00006B/679